Unknown Message

by

Spencer Selby

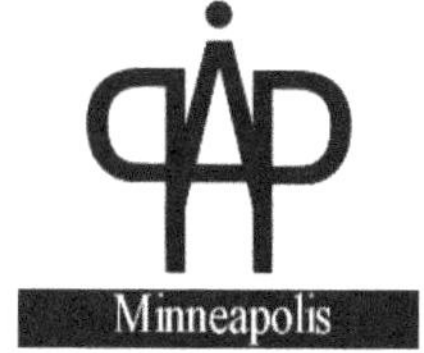

Post-Asemic Press 002

ISBN-13: 978-1-7328788-2-2

Contact: postasemicpress@gmail.com

postasemicpress.blogspot.com

Cover art by Spencer Selby

Design and typesetting by Spencer Selby and David Quiles Guillô

This book is dedicated to Michael Jacobson

Words for UNKNOWN MESSAGE

“Here are some Petri dishes, each full of an alternative writing culture or sample of writing from an alternative civilization. Some of this writing appears to have been yanked and stretched, as if it had been written on a sheet of elastic material. Other pages resemble maps, diagrams, digital crystals, tattoo designs or ancient pictographs. Noise or wind or smeariness is a common feature. Throughout this work, the third dimension seems to be trying to push itself forward from the flat paper surface. There's a human presence hiding on one page, perhaps the author hard at work. I suggest that this book contains a message from the future.”

—Tim Gaze

“The physical act of reading is altered here, it undergoes a shift. The challenge is to assess how a reader views and how the veiwer reads. A sentence carries information from one margin to the other. The line travels across the page. What happens between margins is open to interpretation, to some divine corruption. In UNKNOWN MESSAGE, Selby not only adjusts the content of the line and how it reaches a margin, but he takes alphabet to new visual potentials. Meaning is in the seeing meaning form new ways of seeing. These poems are derived from visual chromatin conveying the genetic material of a future language event. Again, the cycle of disintegration to renewal in visual language approaches. These asemic missives find you, are awaiting your attention.”

—Nico Vassilakis

"Fuzzy-wuzzy, cranky, cryptic, vibrant, prickly, deterritorialized, endearing... no, these are not names of Snow White's avant-garde dwarves but just a few adjectives that adhere to the overwhelming variety of Spencer Selby's asemic marvels. These textural, textilic surfaces invite engagement of the most tactile kind, but they can't be touched except with our loving, delighted eyes. Poring over them is a wild ride into the possibilities of illumination and meaning. If Plato's cave were the ideal rather than the simulacrum, its walls would feature these brilliant marvels. We are drawn toward these angelic morsels of signification, flickering sememes that reveal and conceal."

—Maria Damon

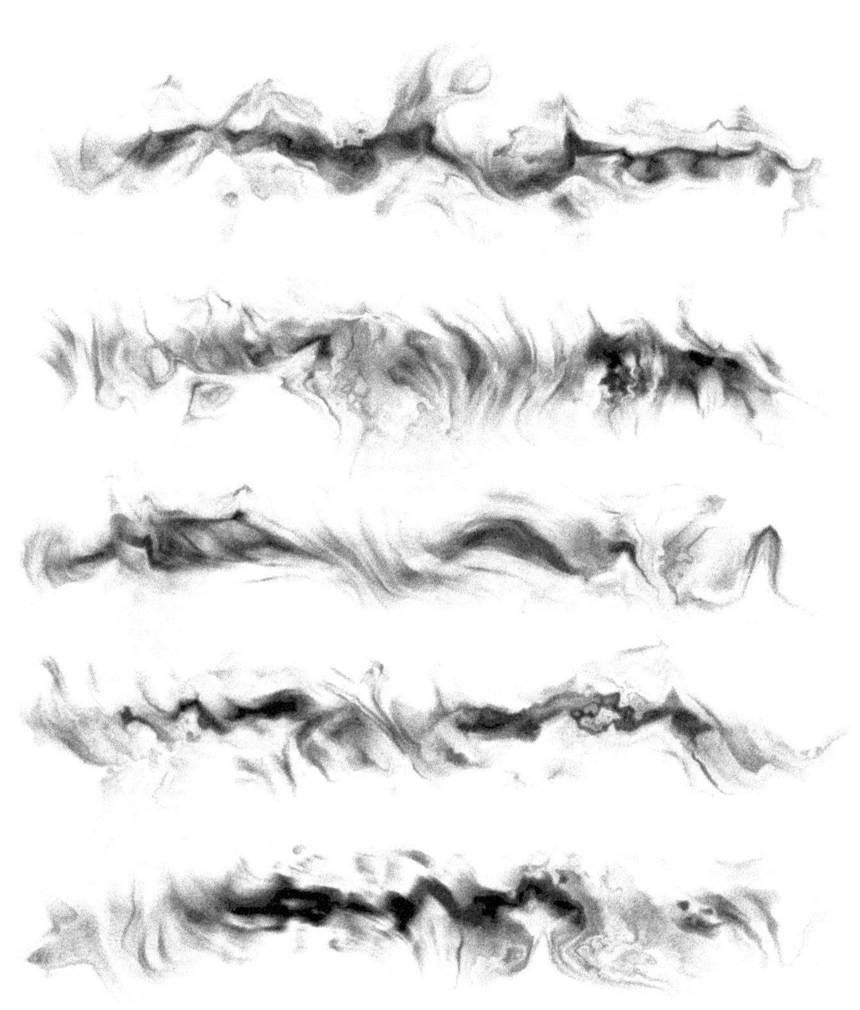

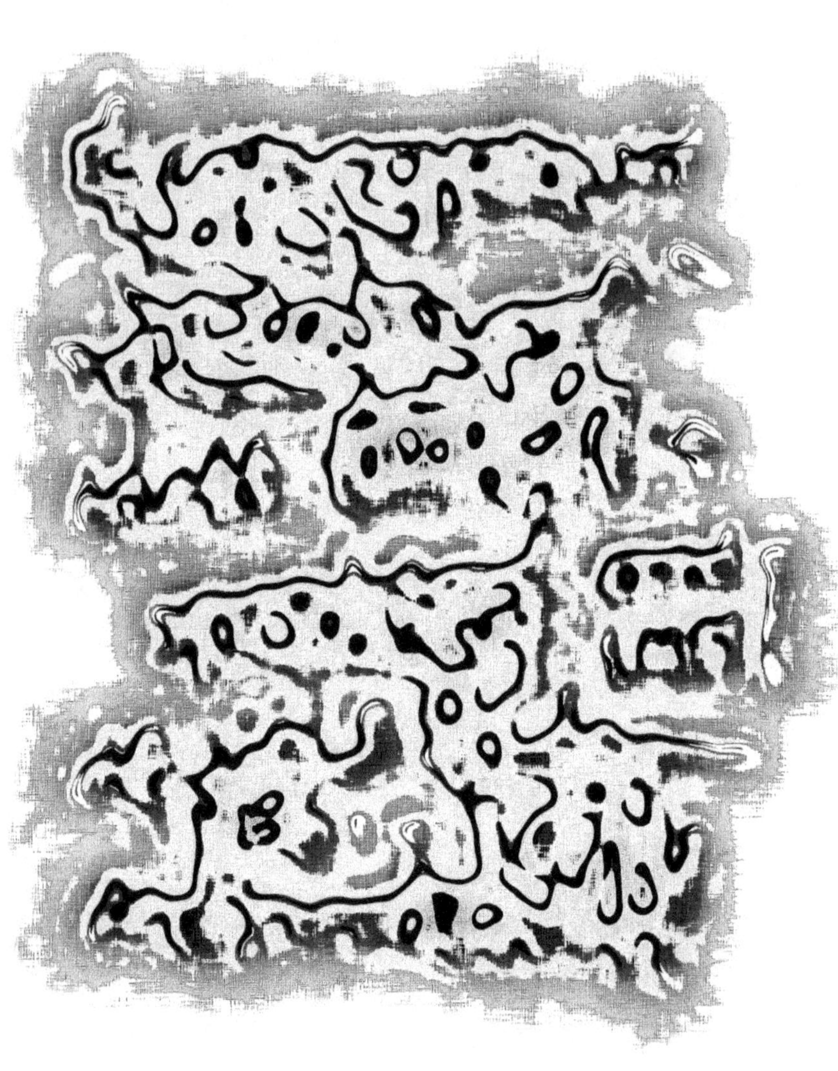

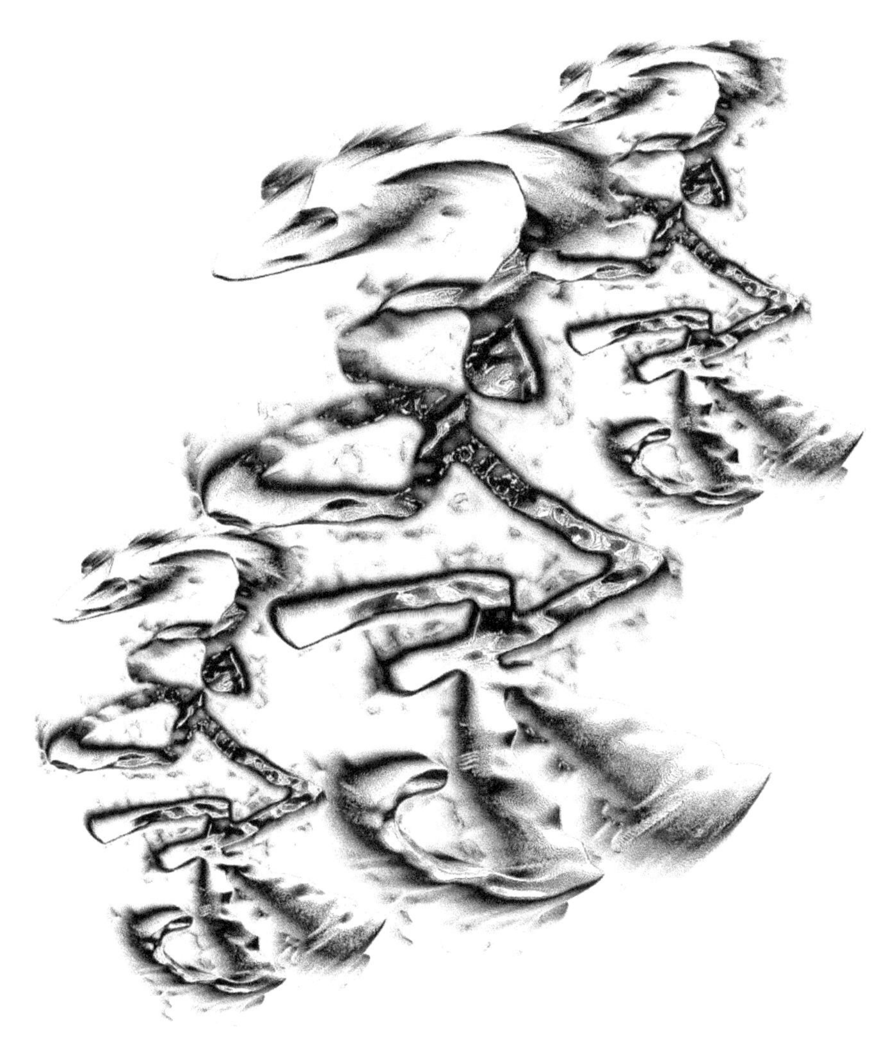

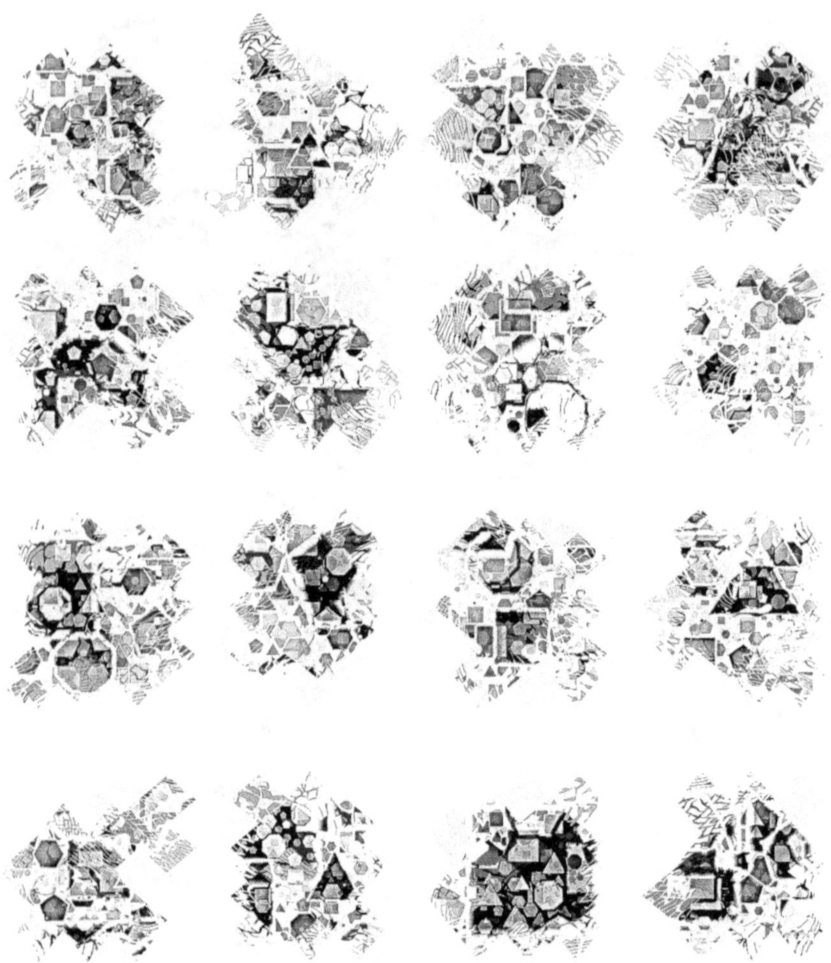

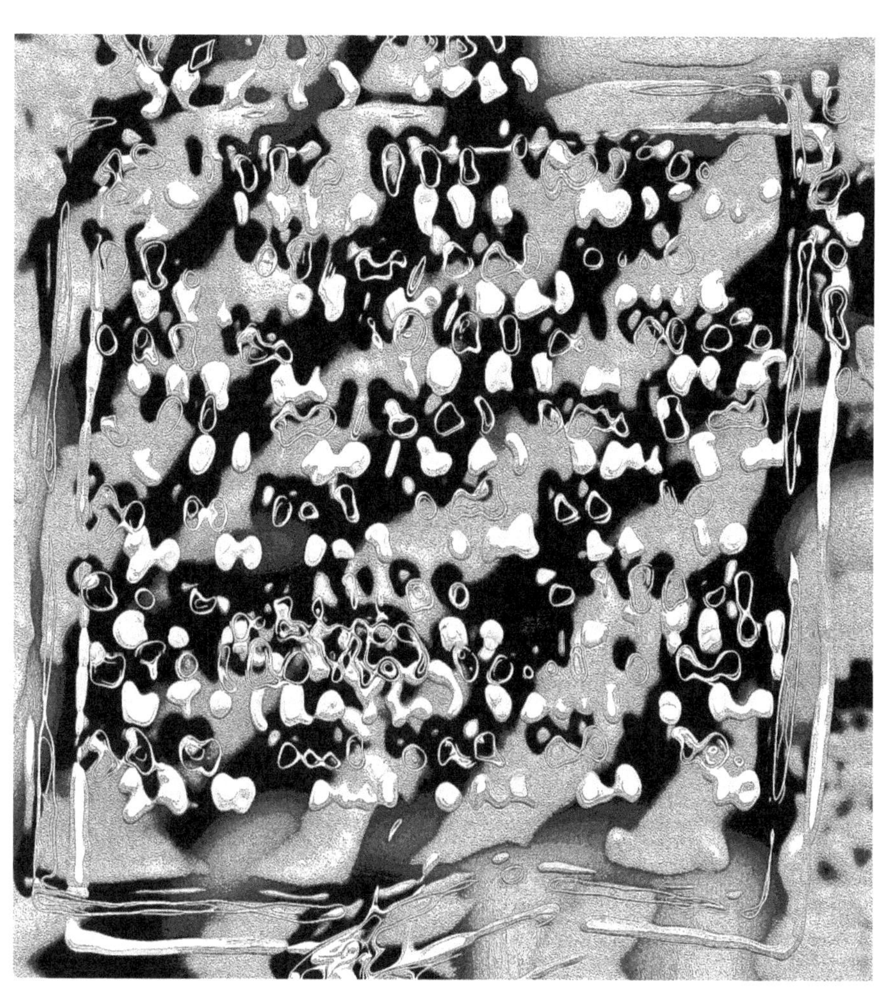

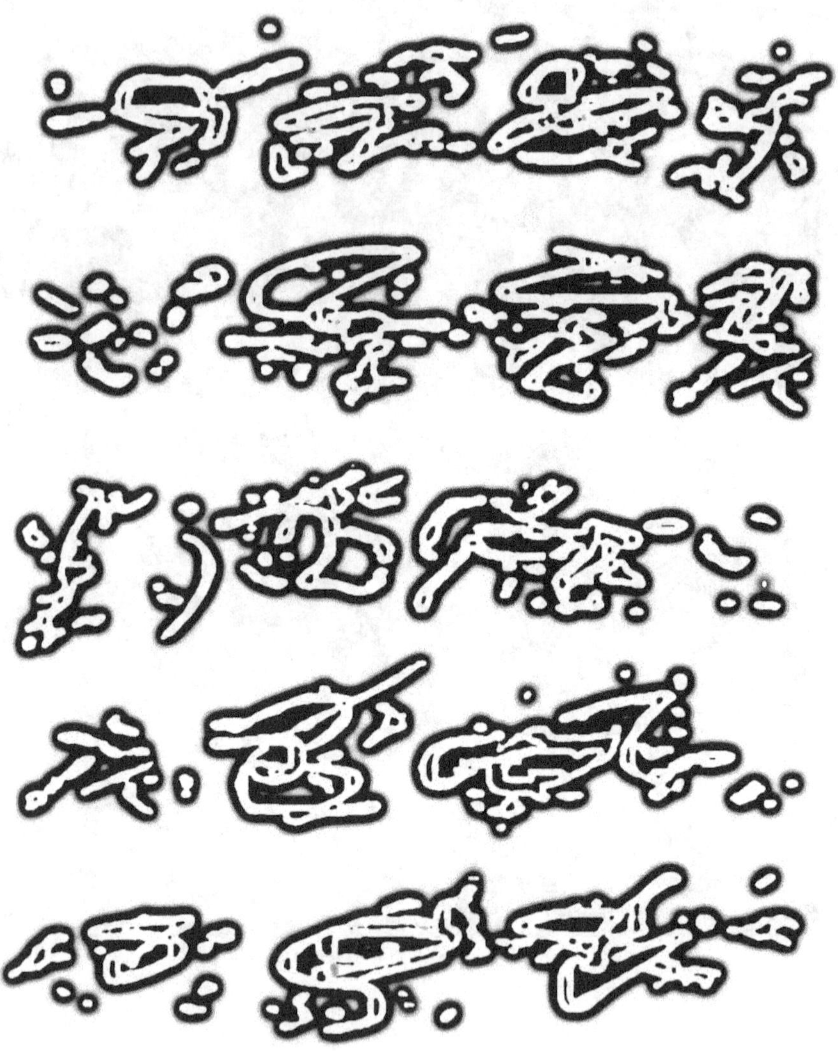

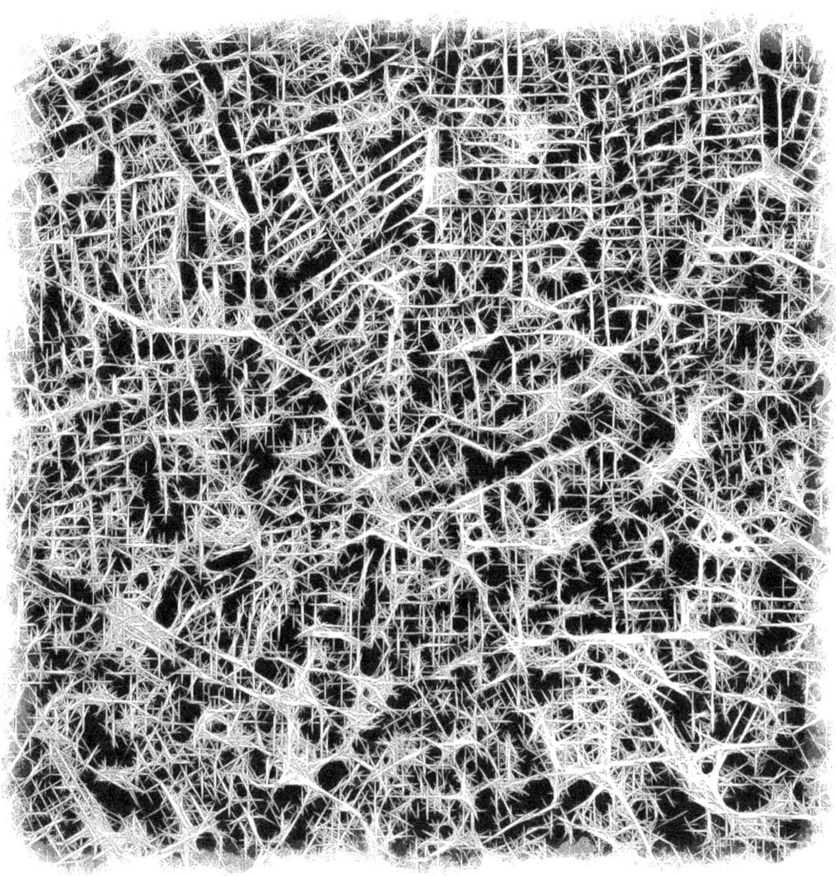

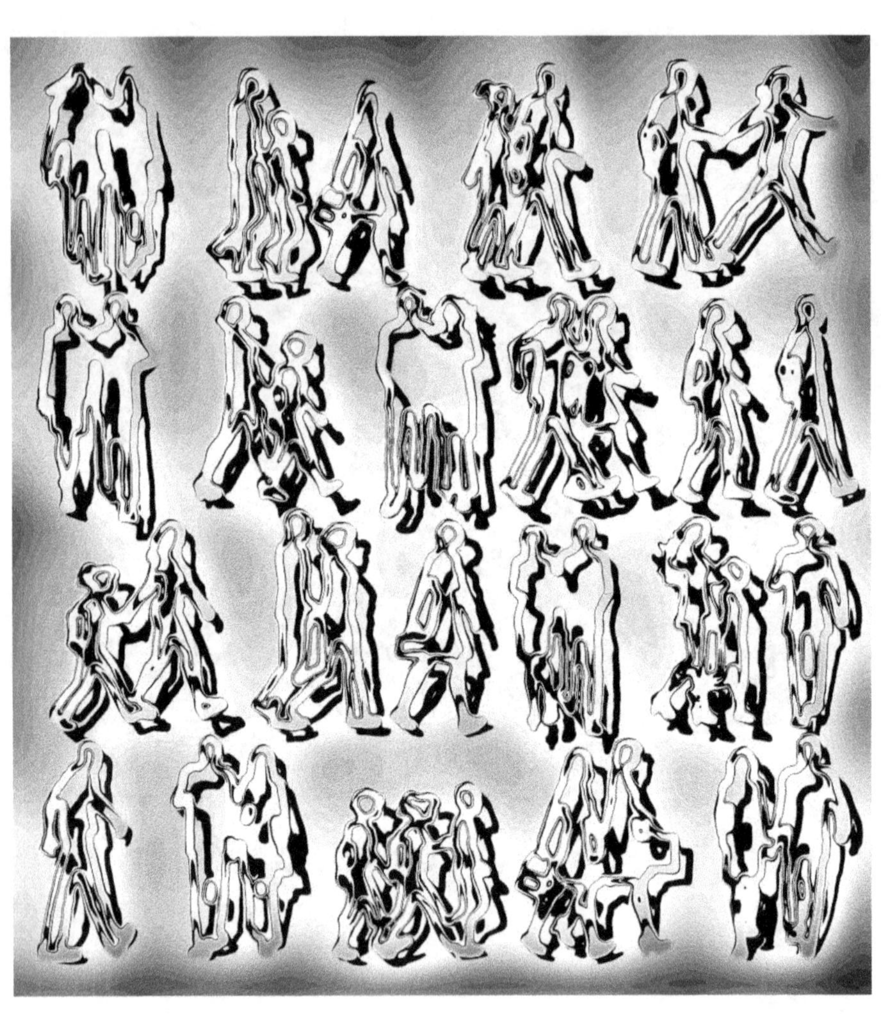

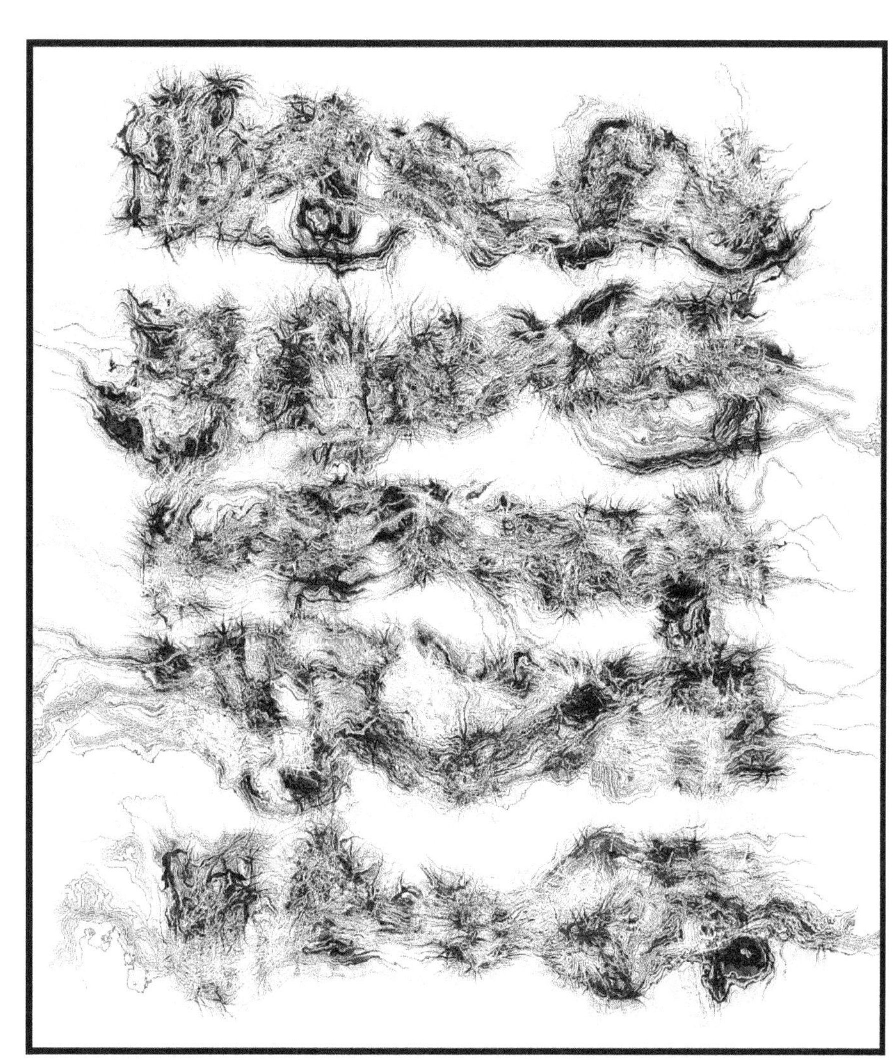

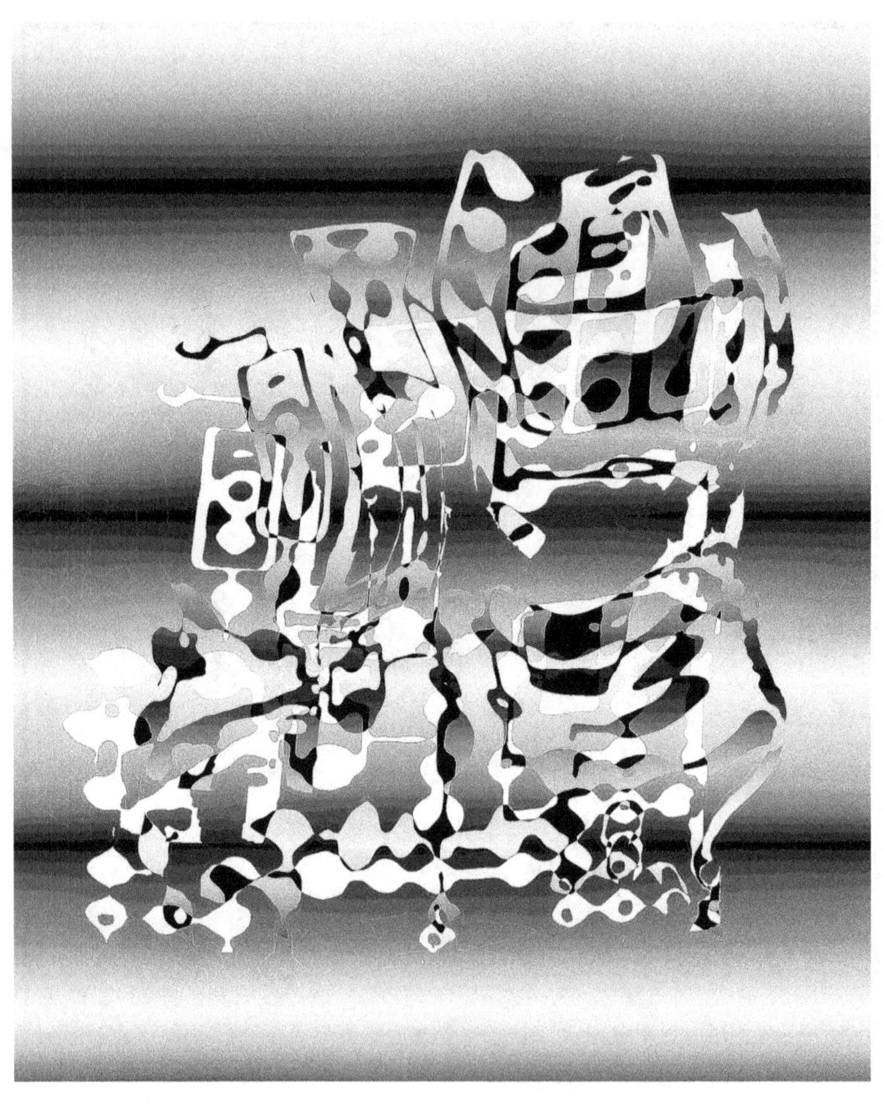

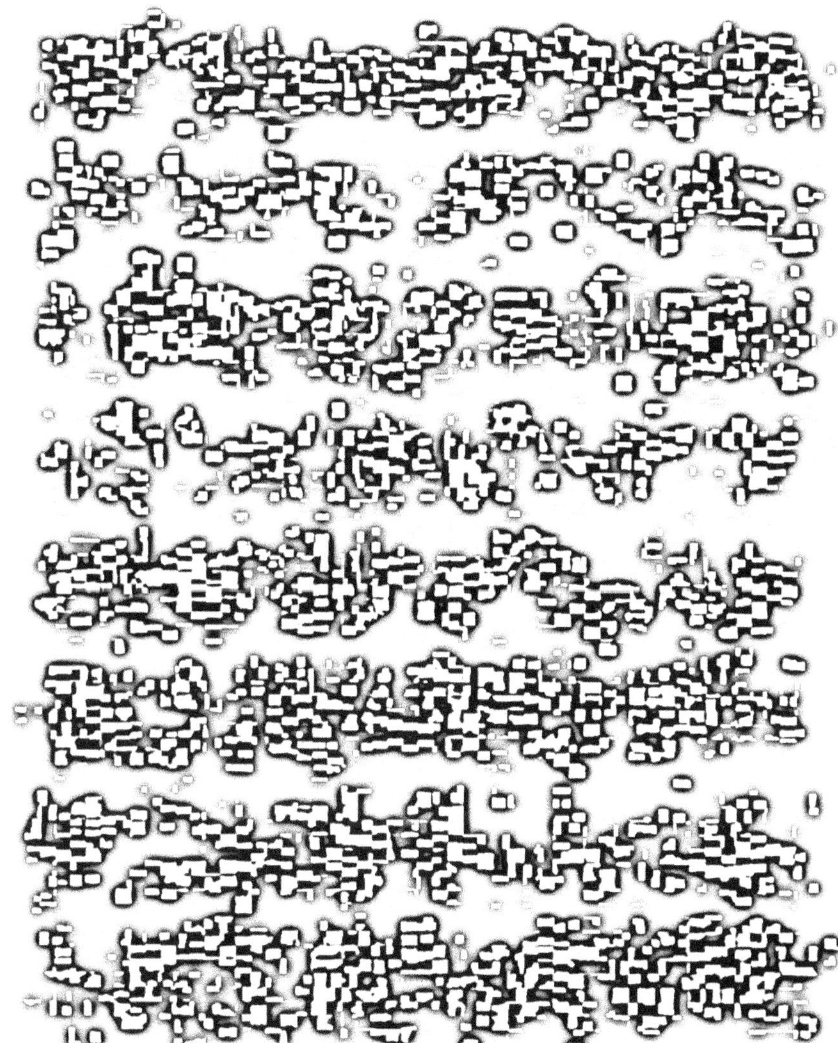

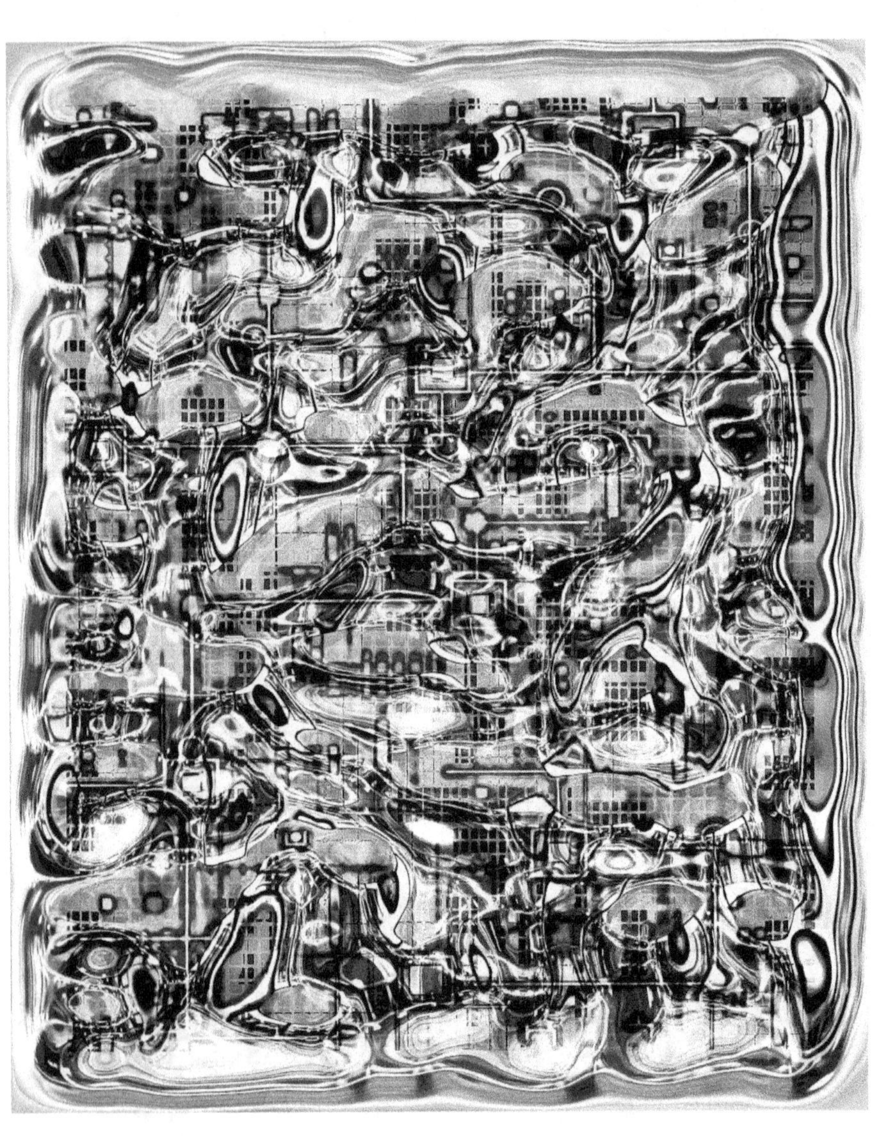

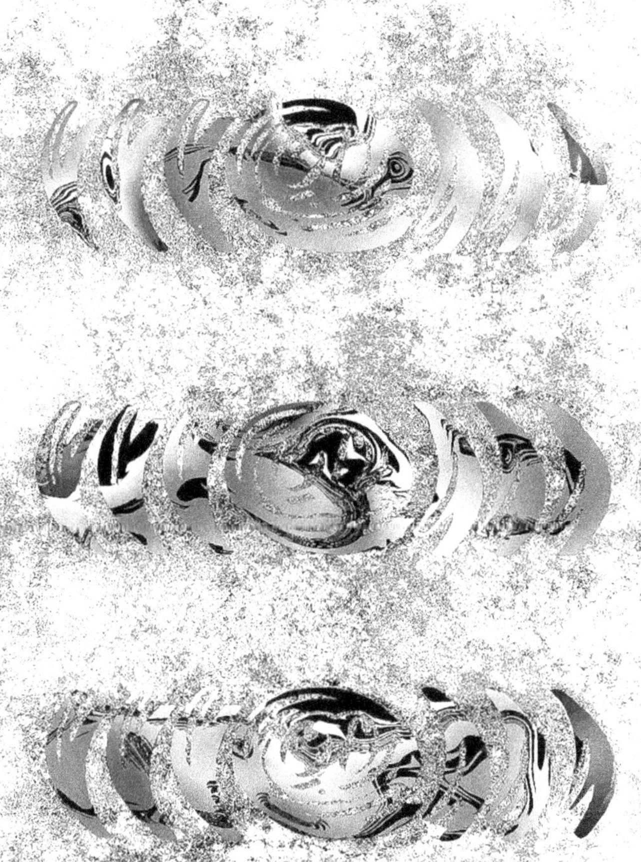

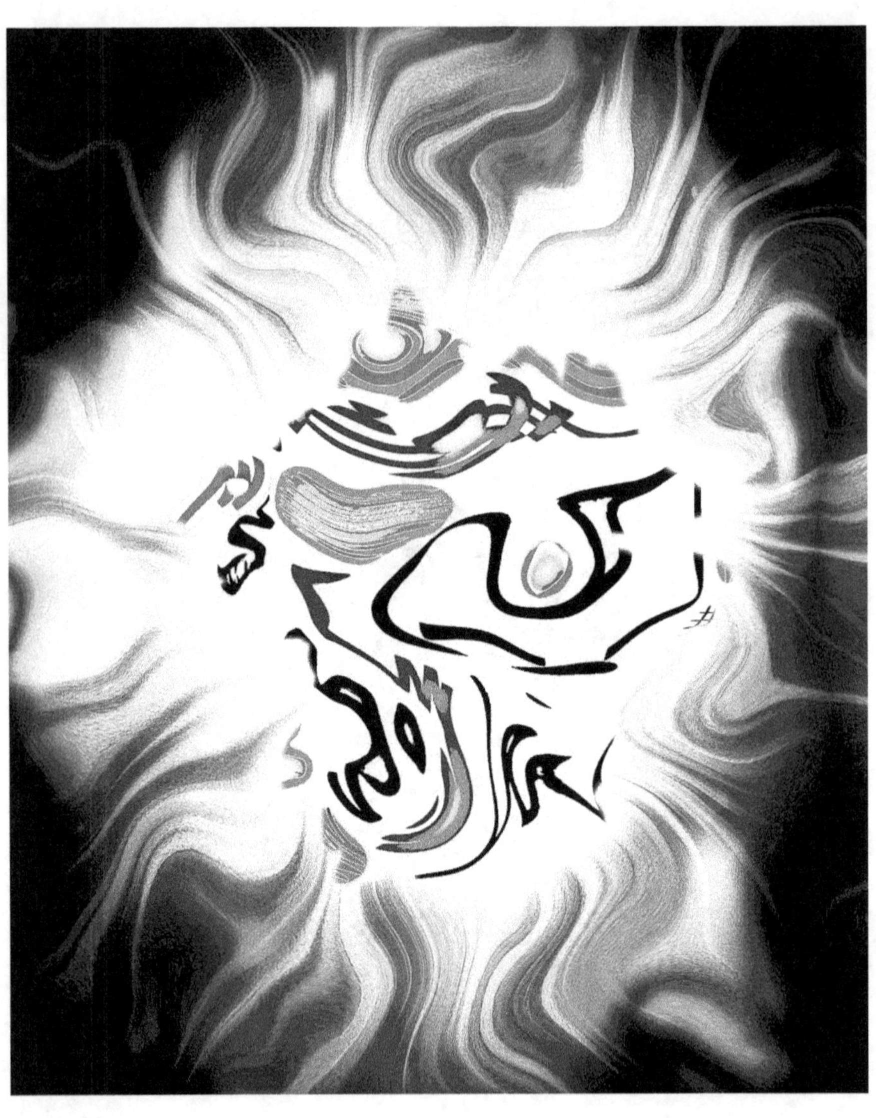

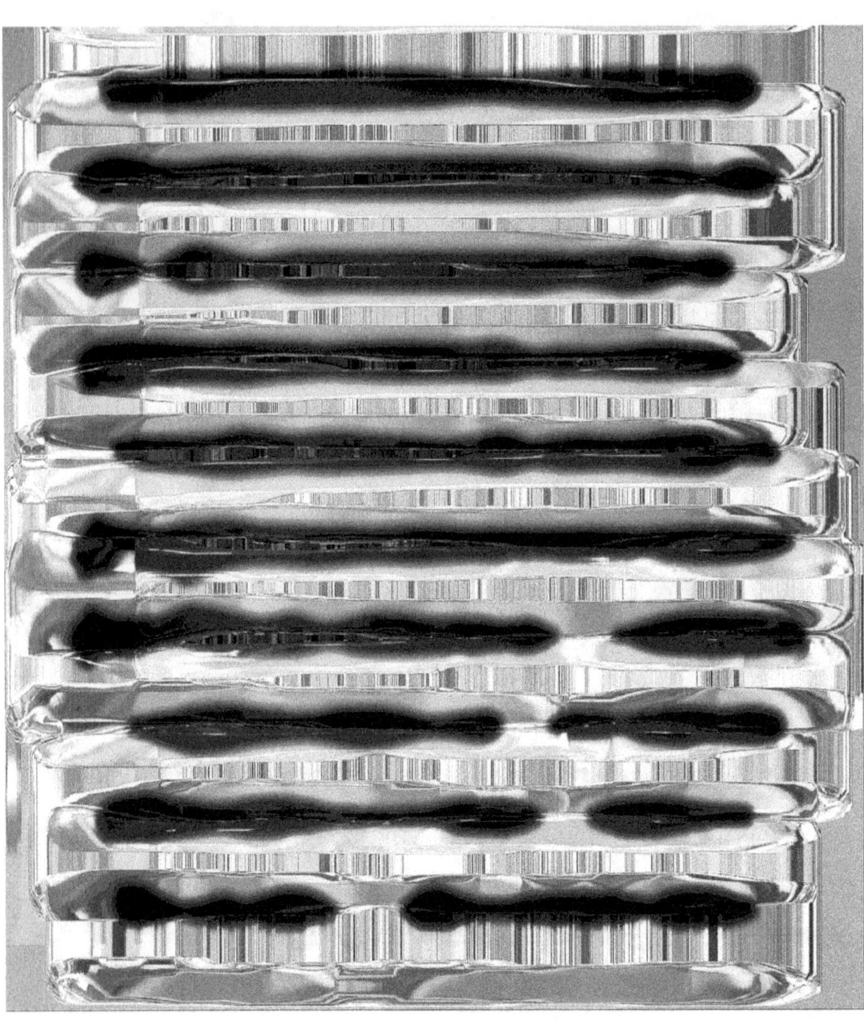

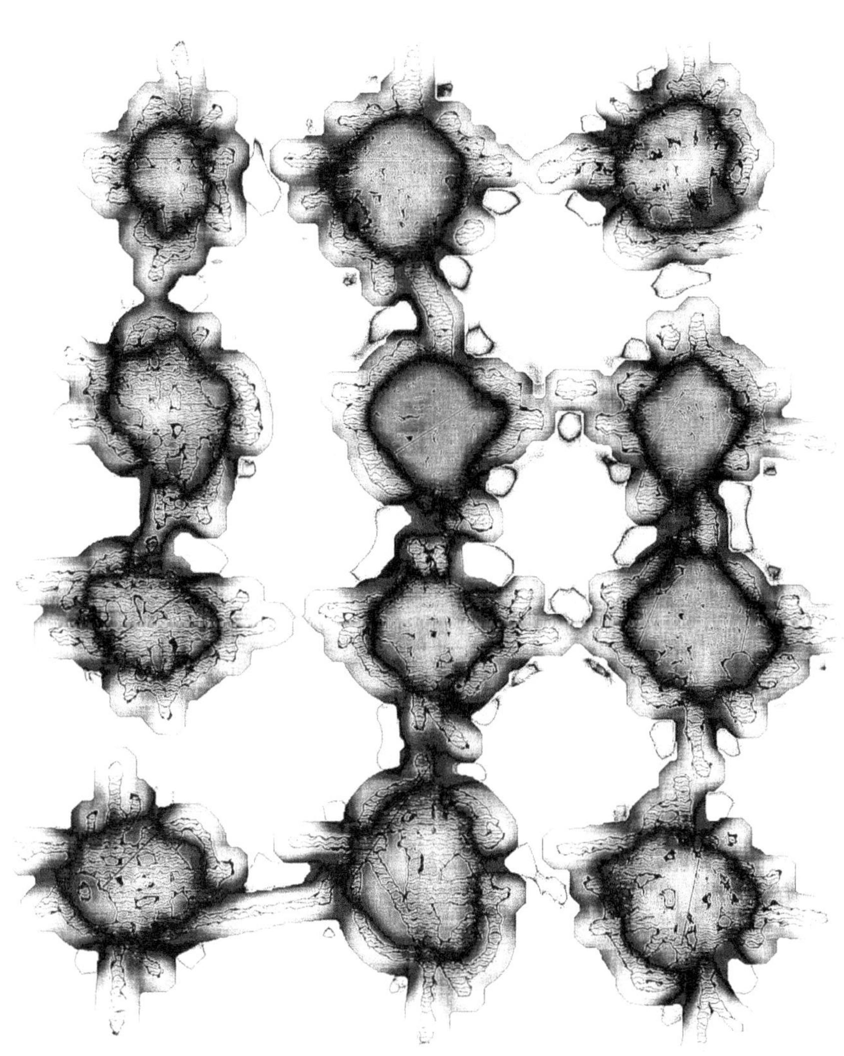

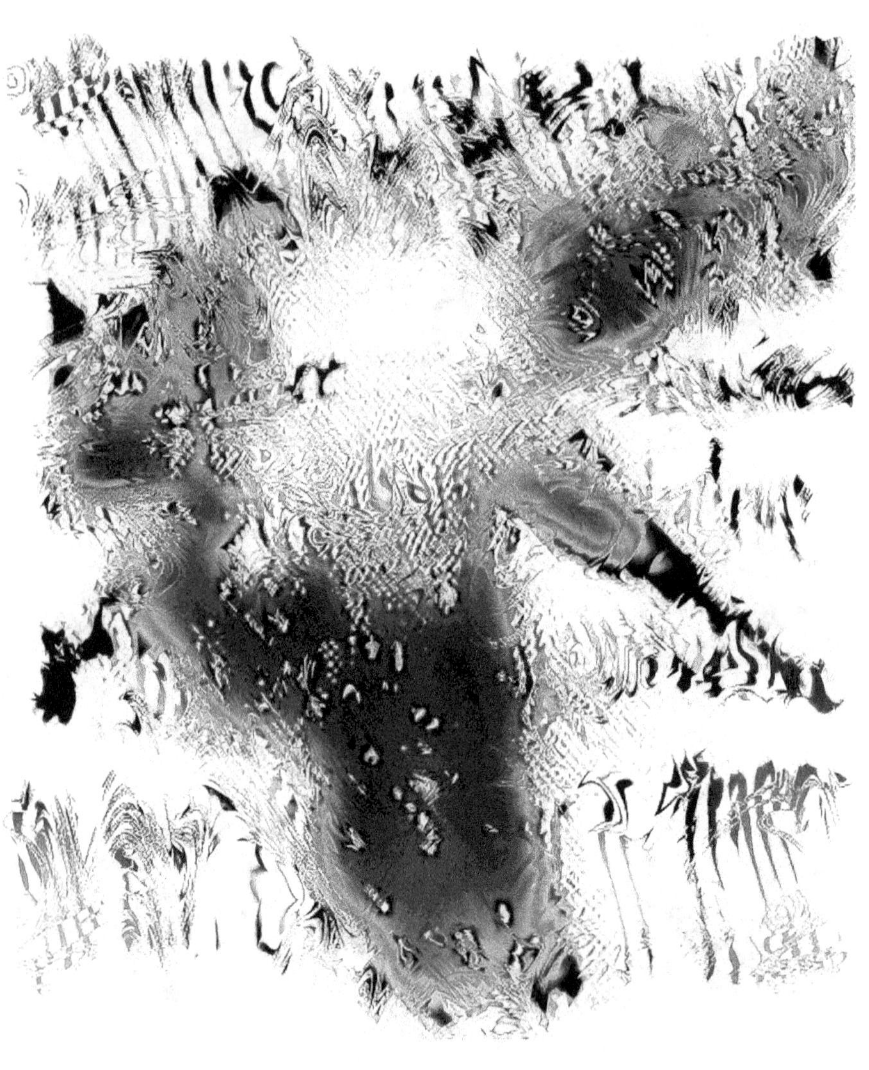

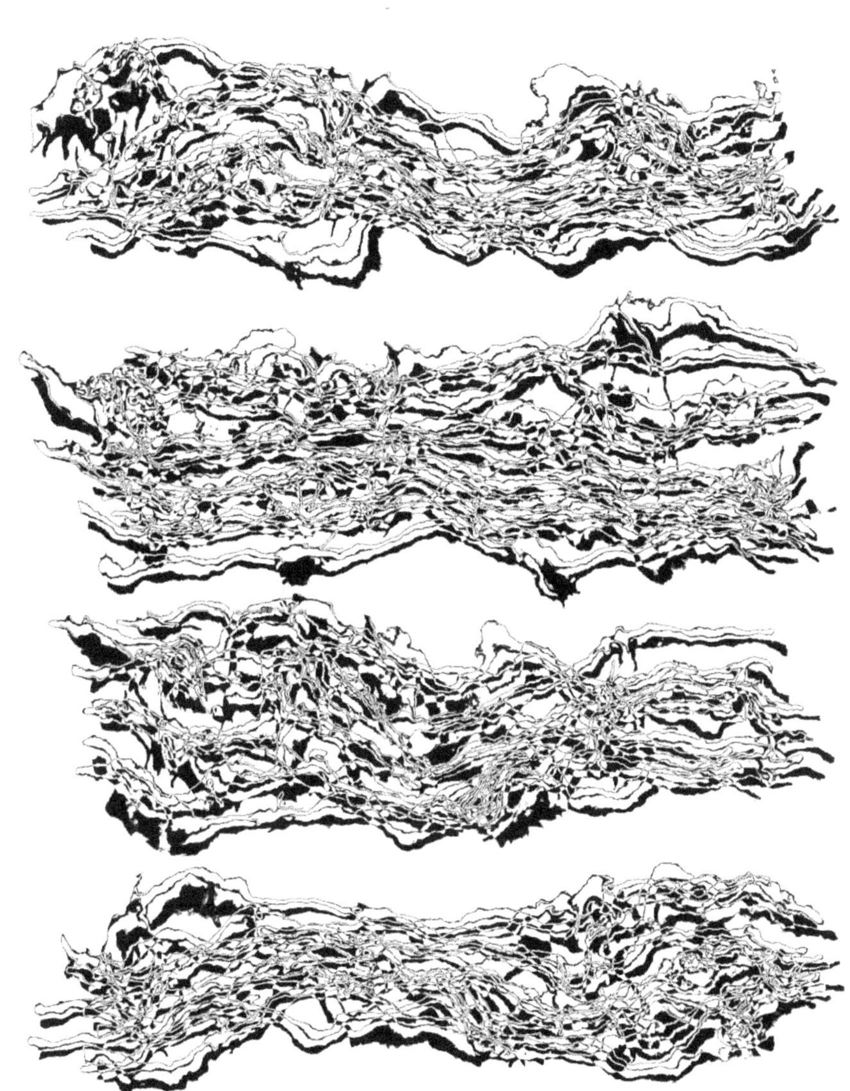

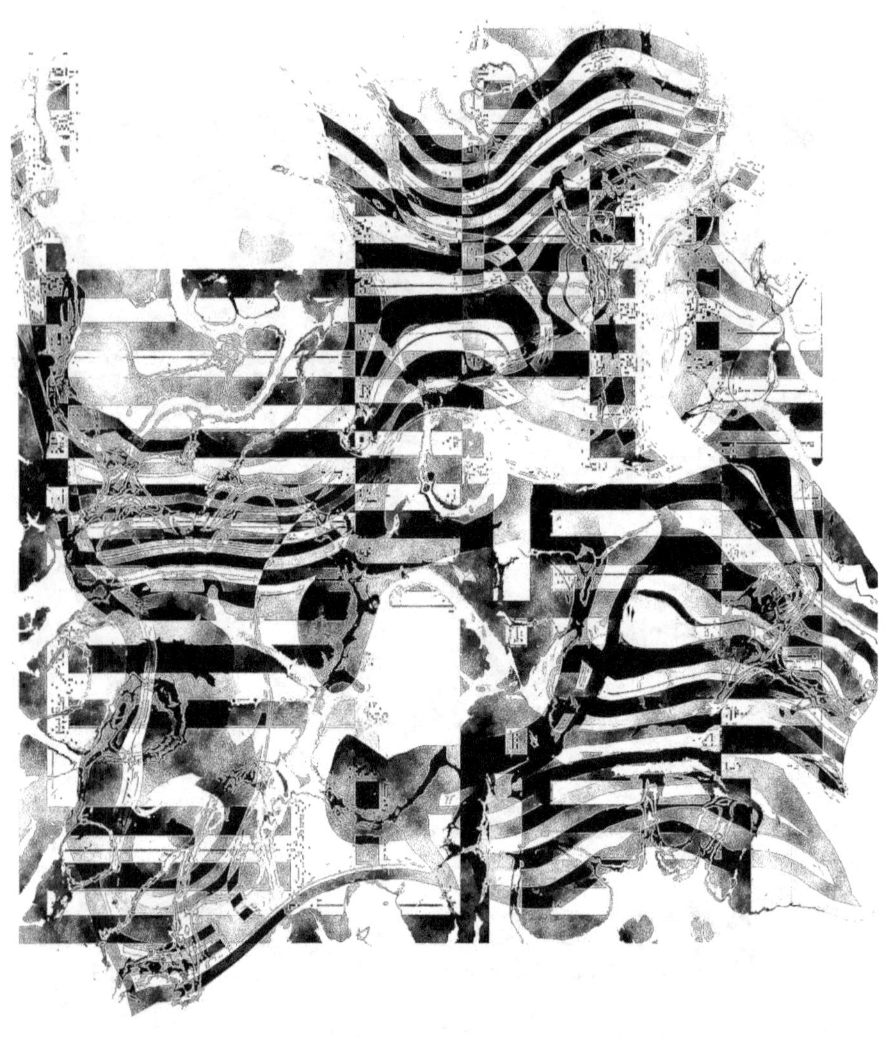

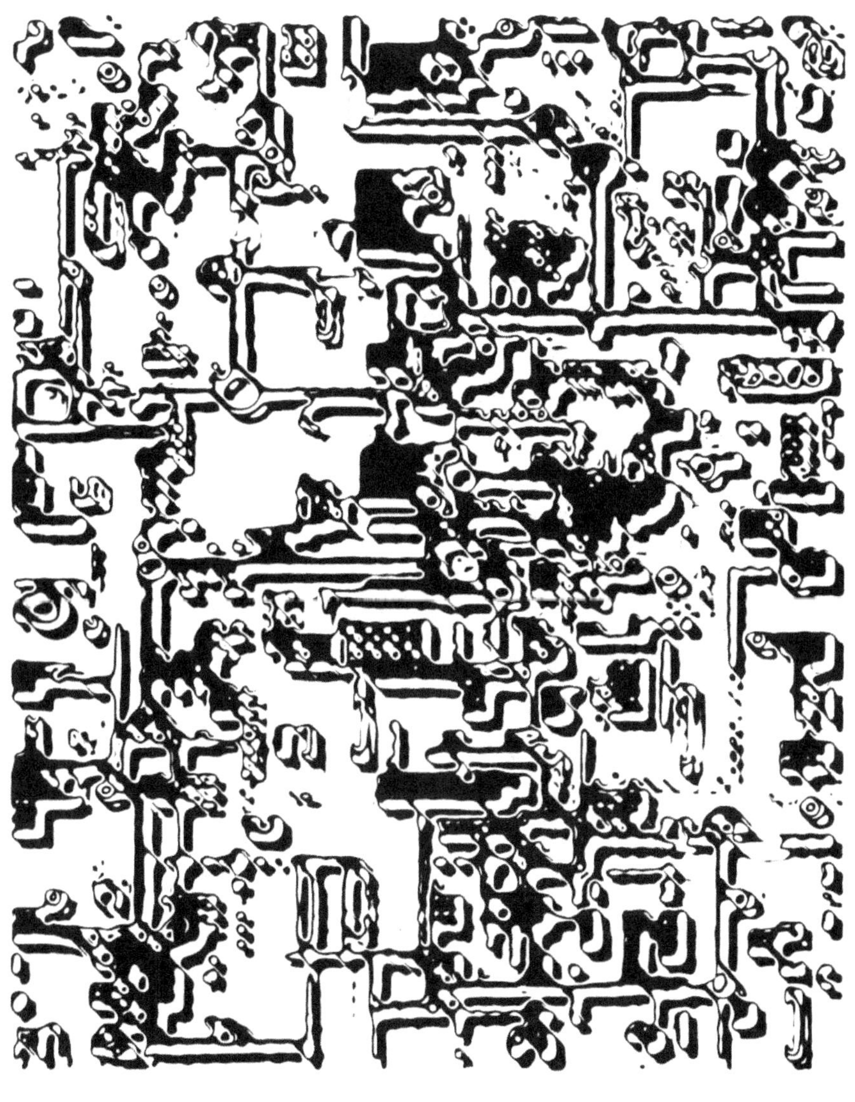

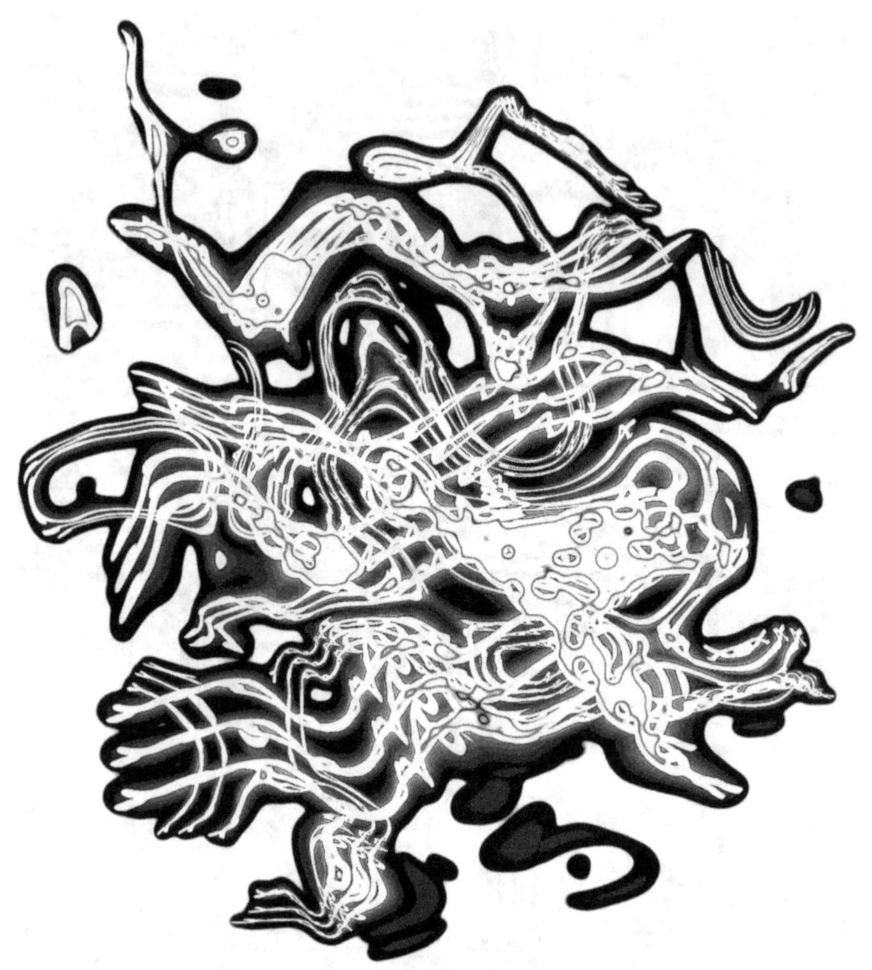

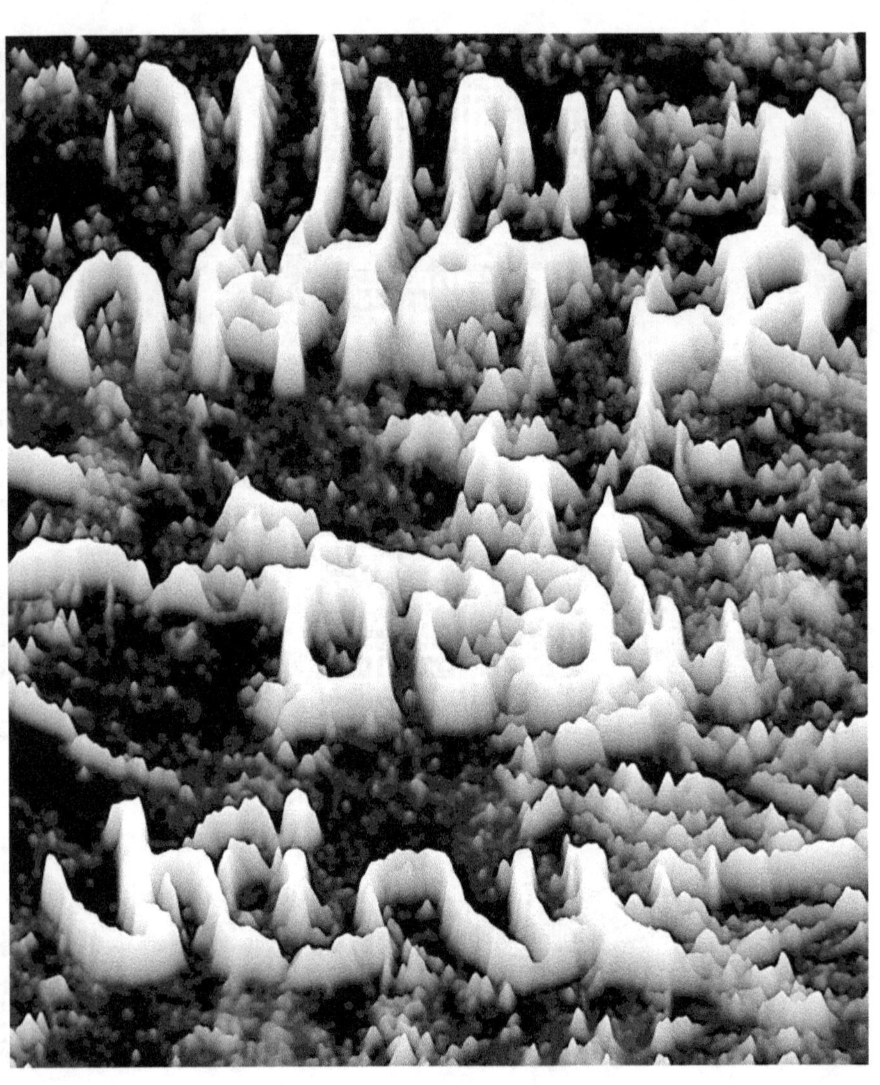

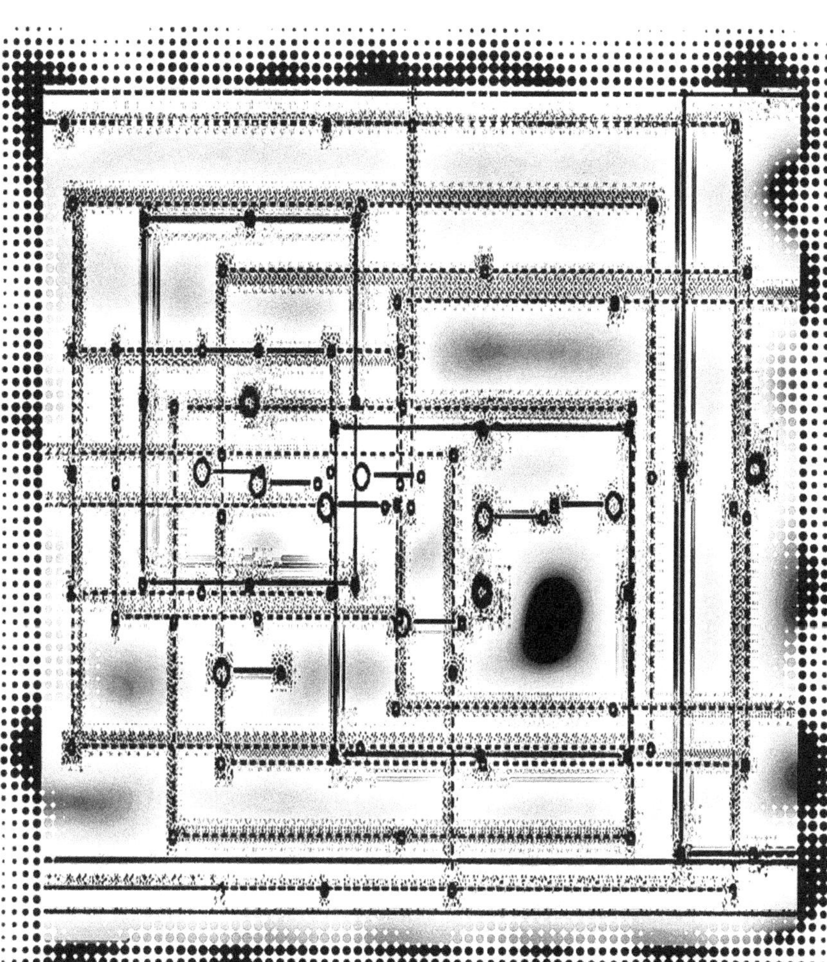

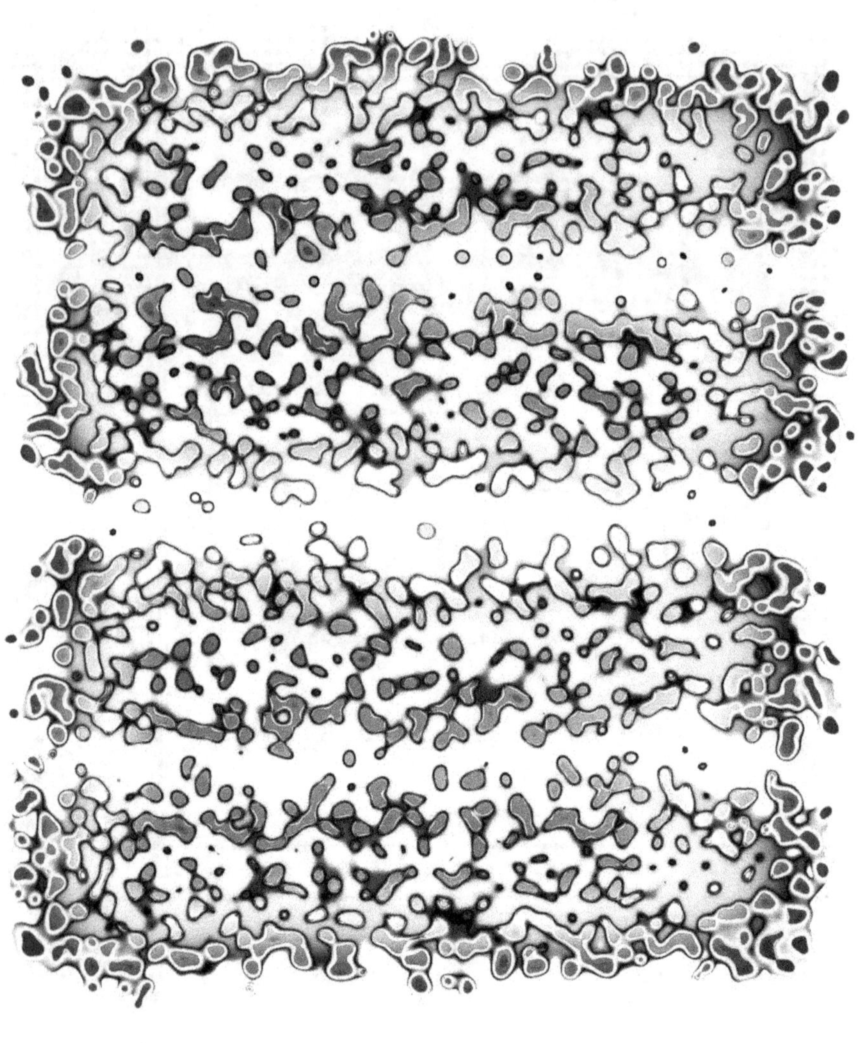

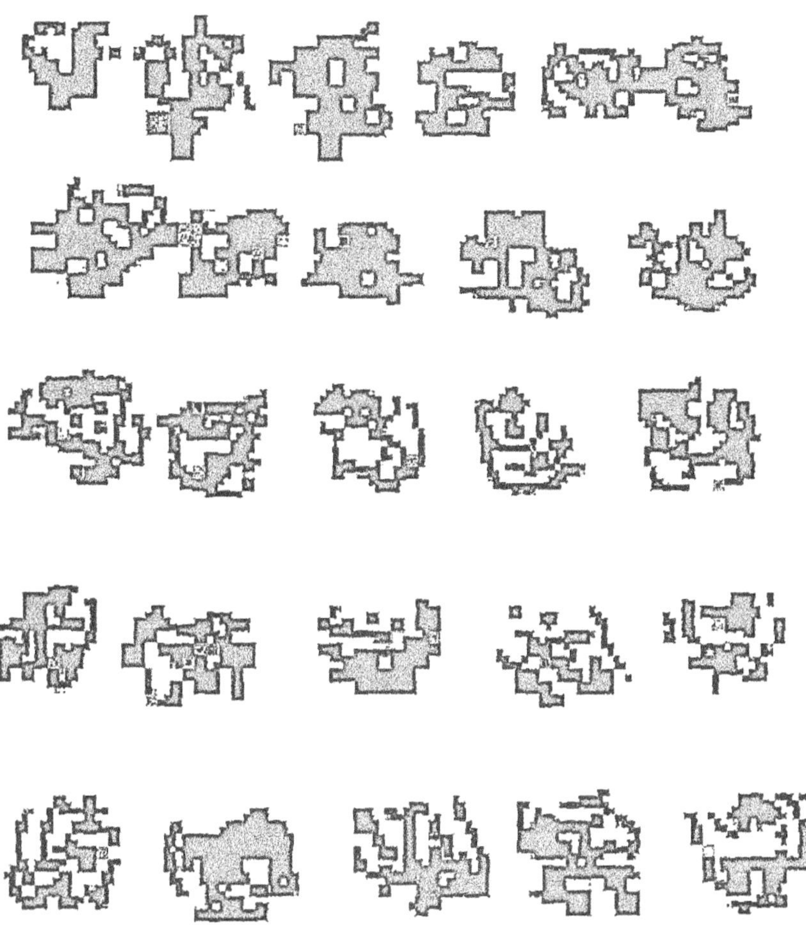

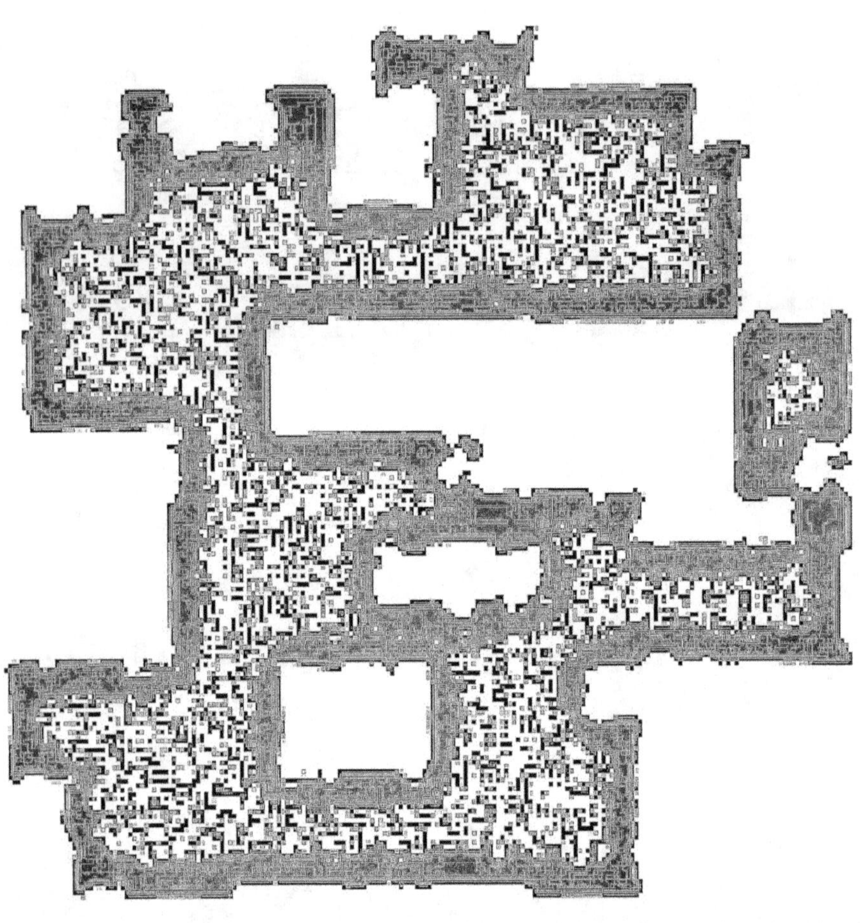

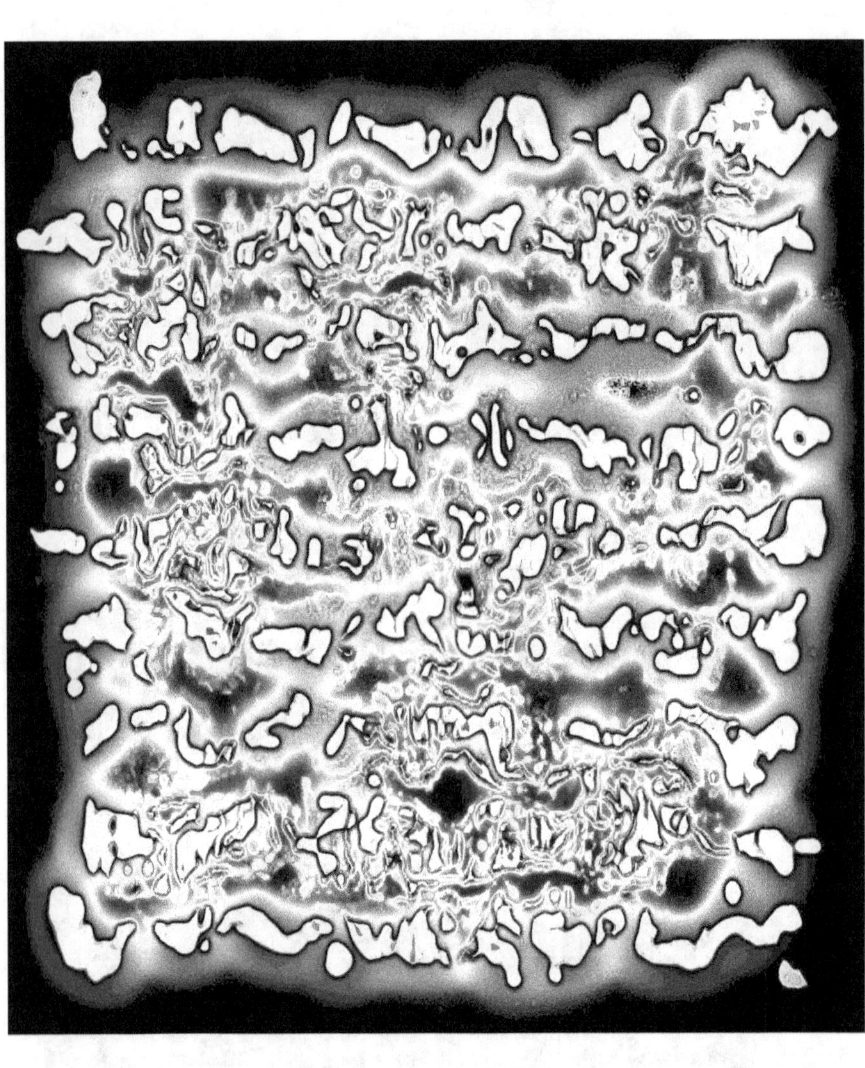

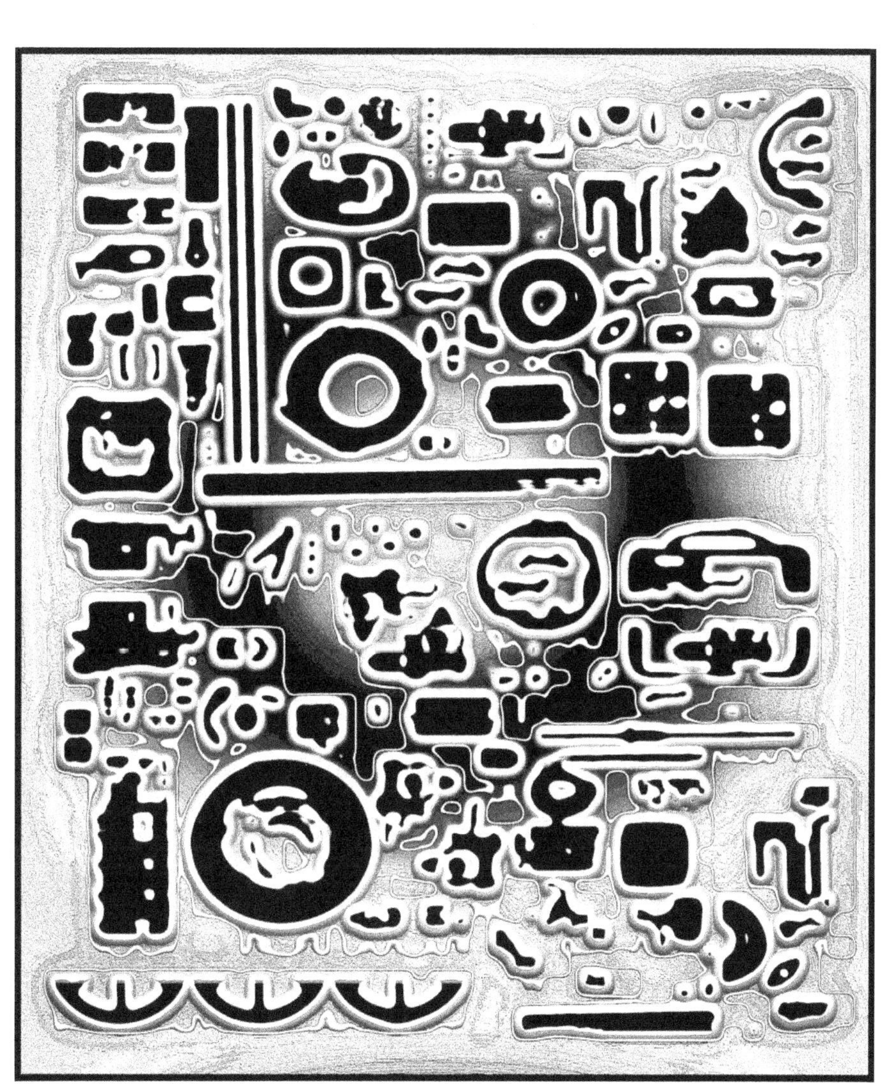

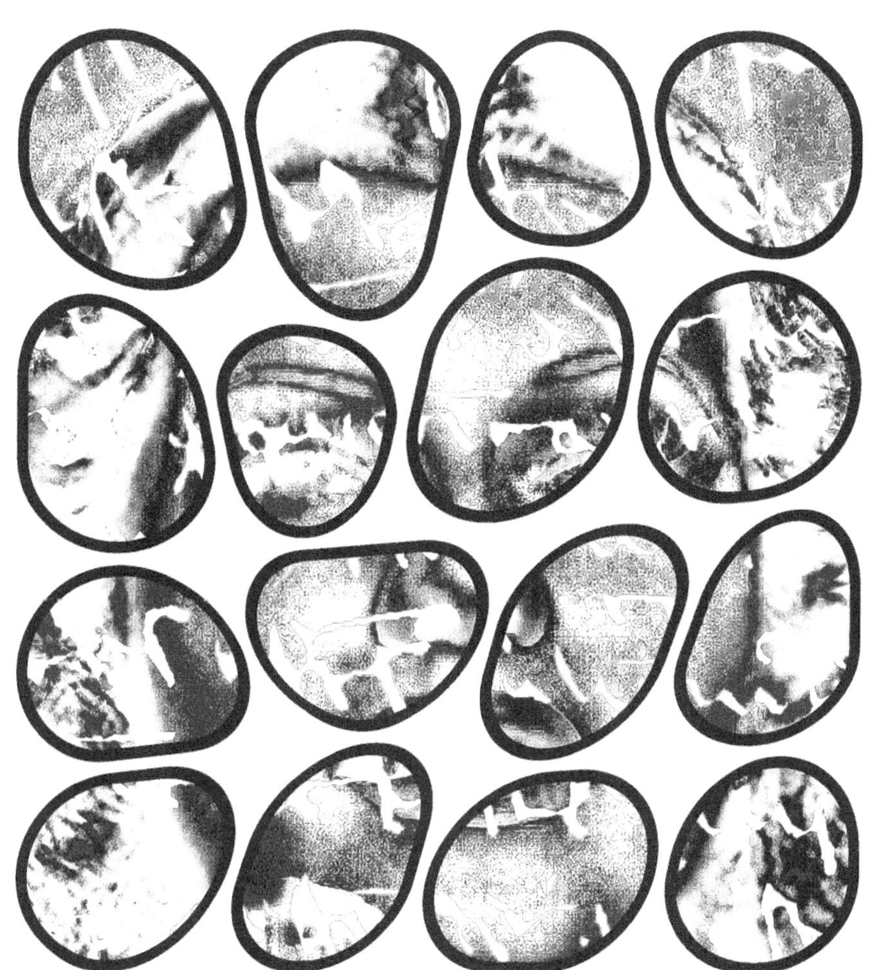

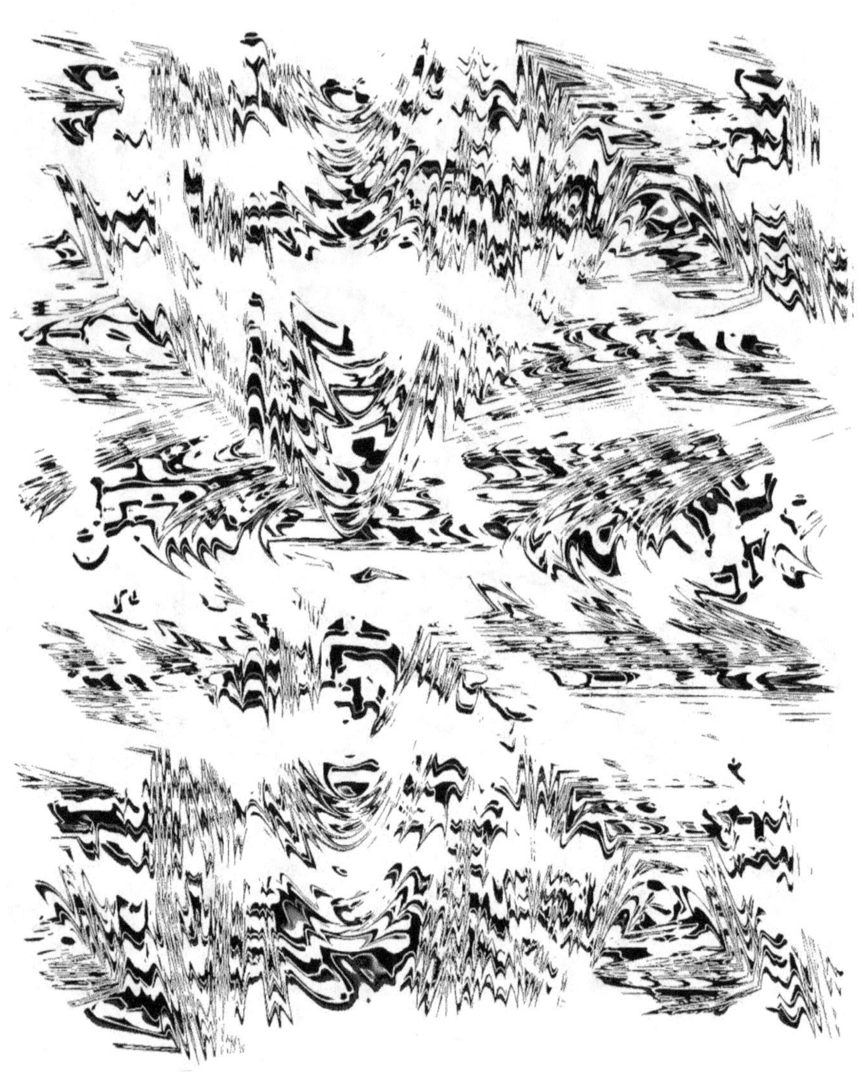

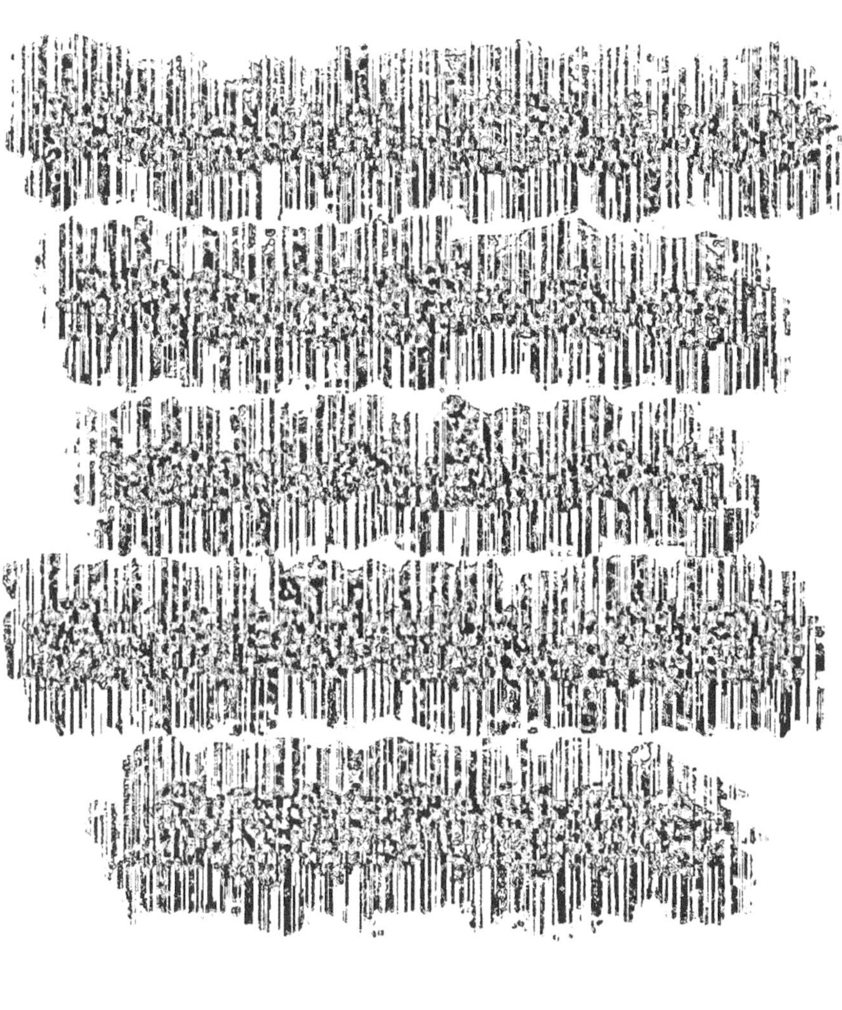

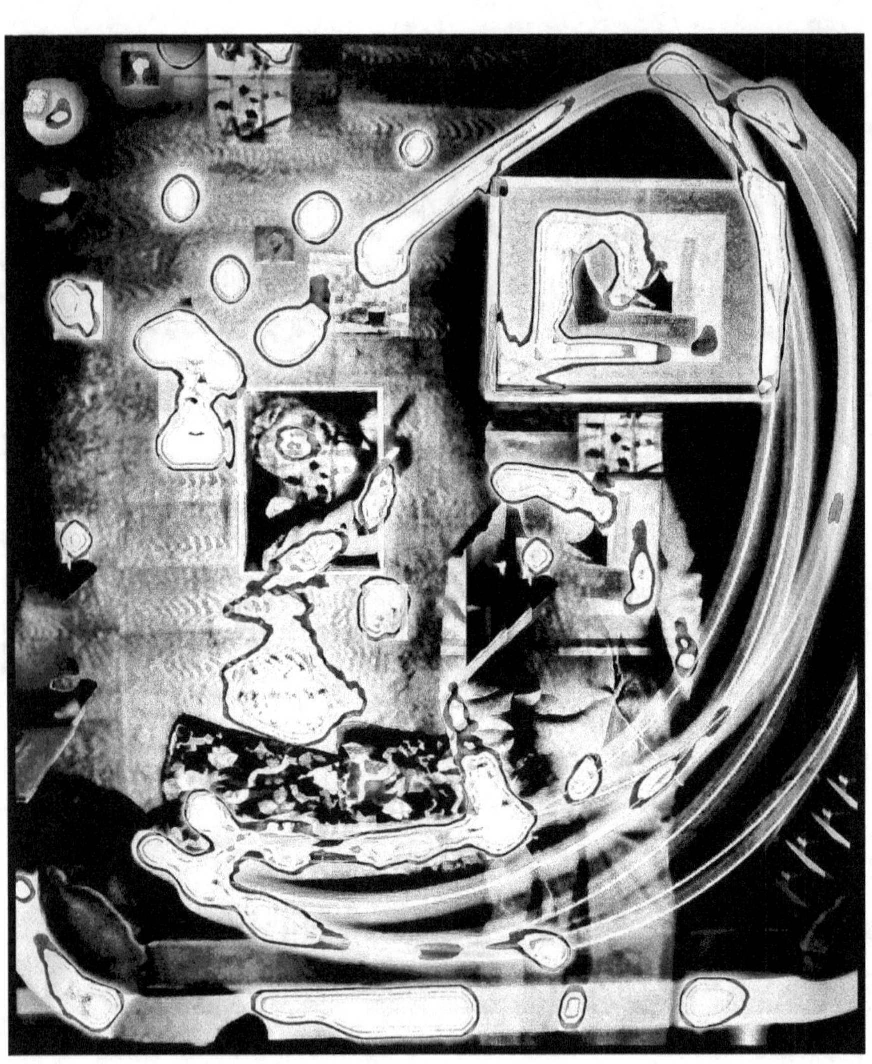

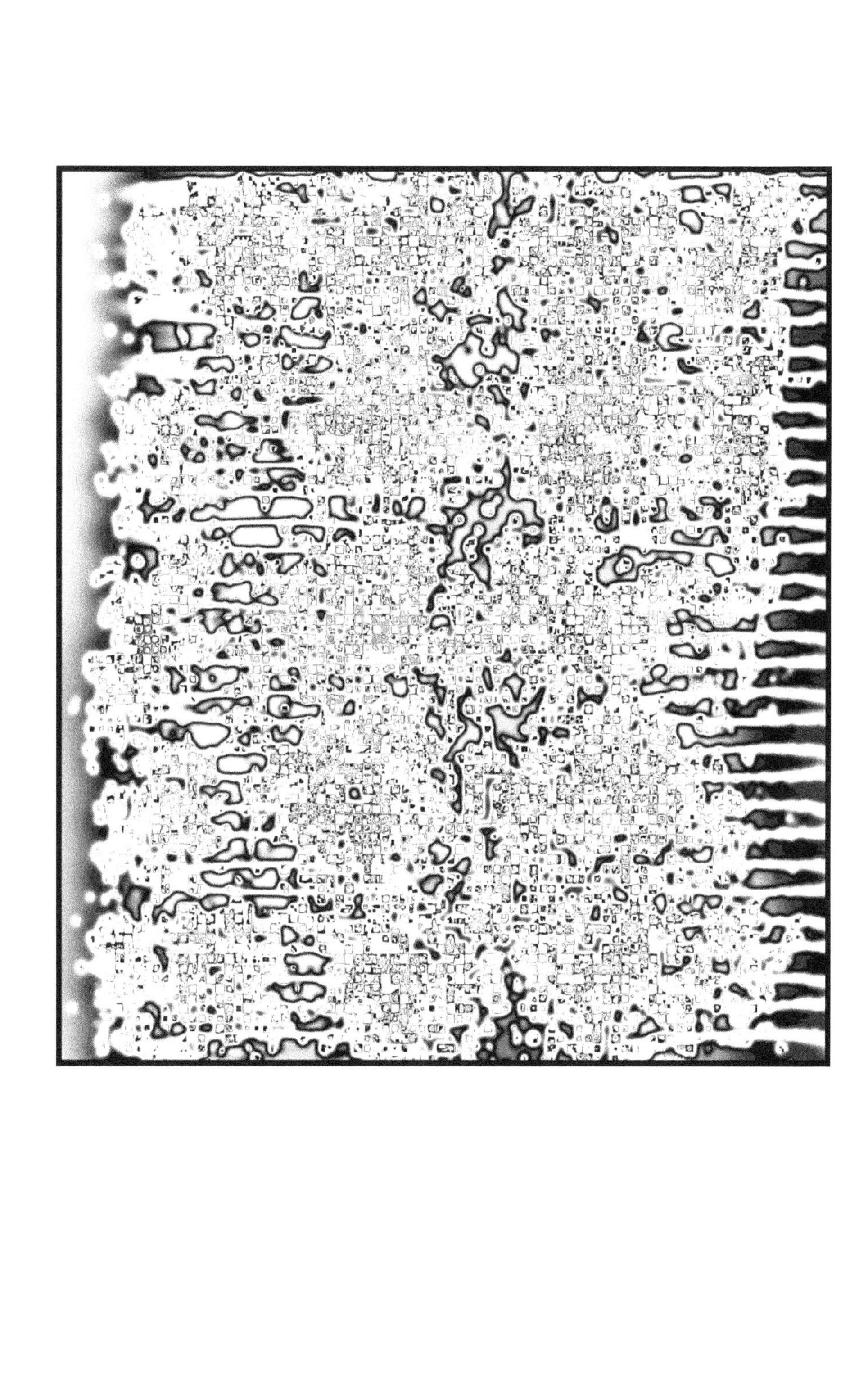

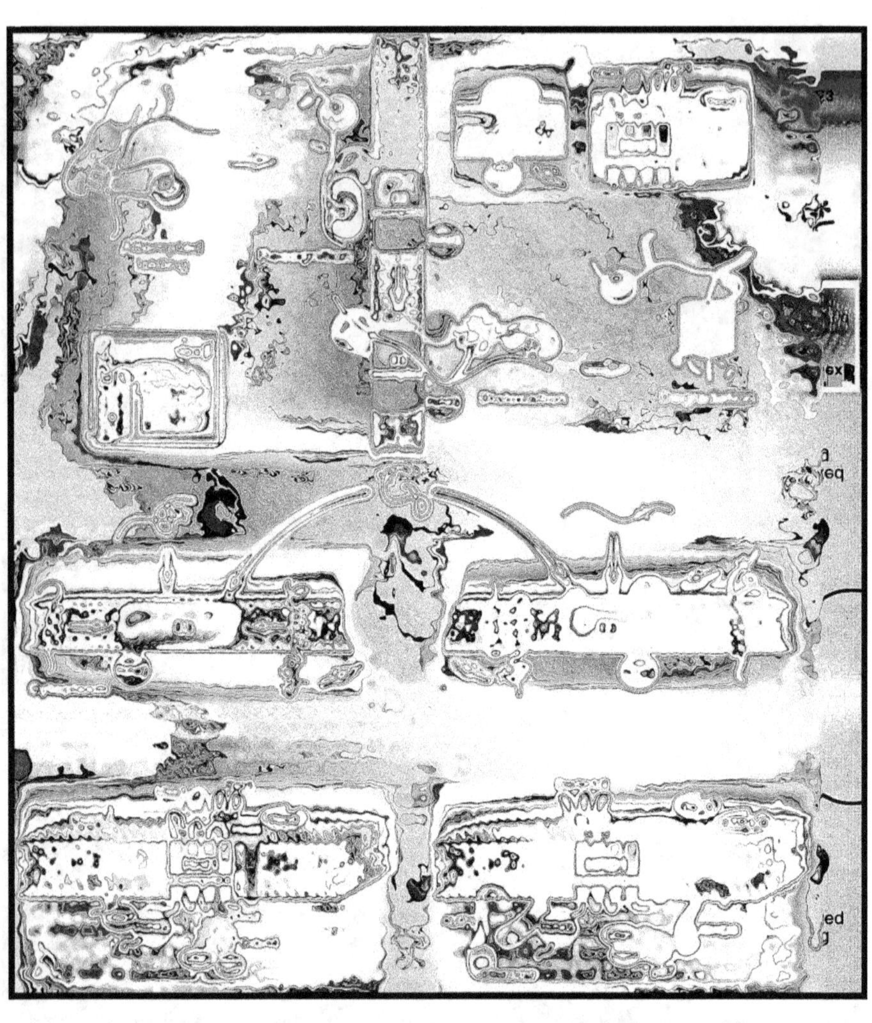

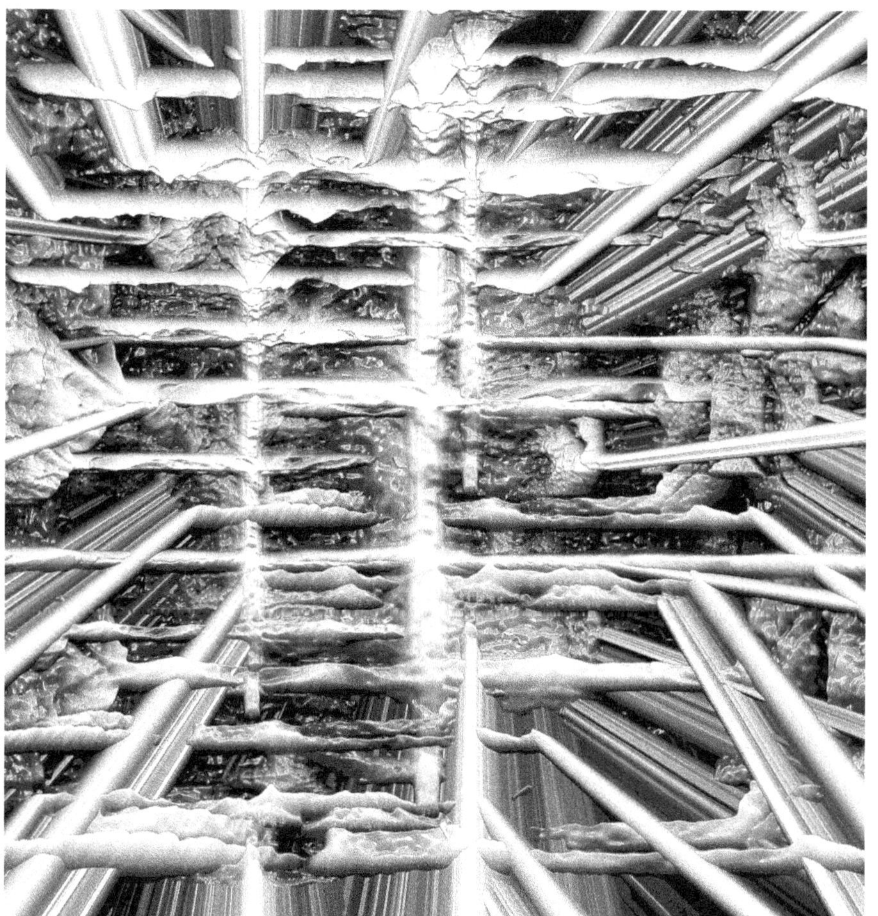

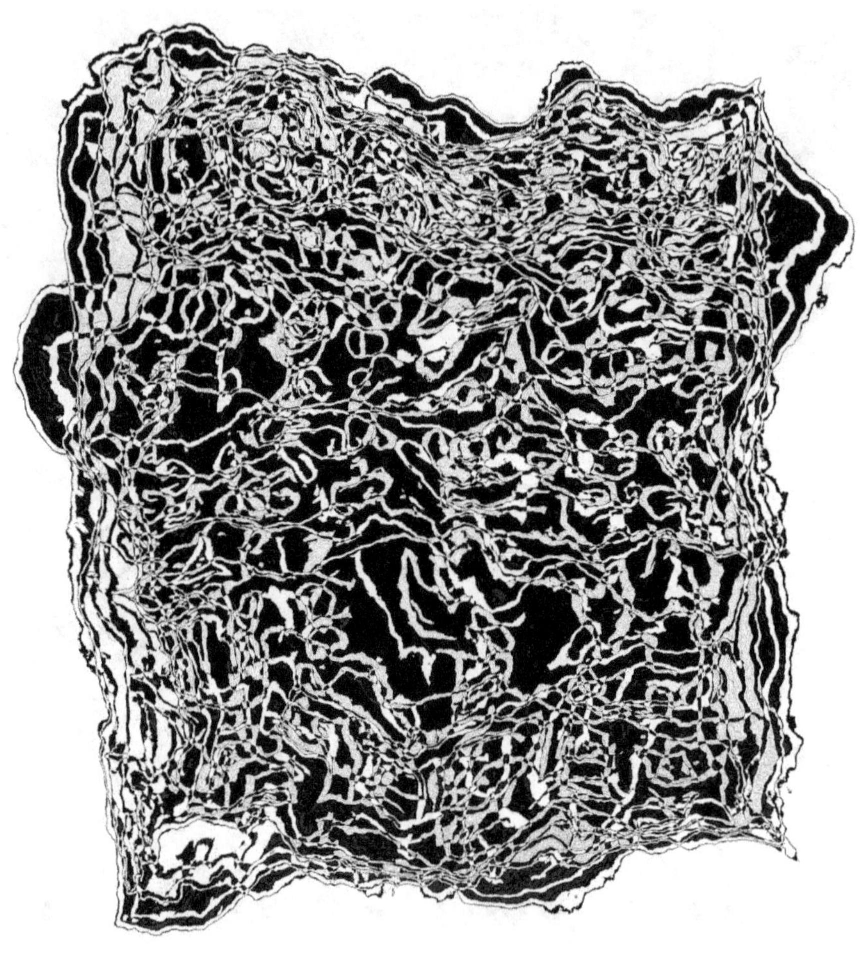

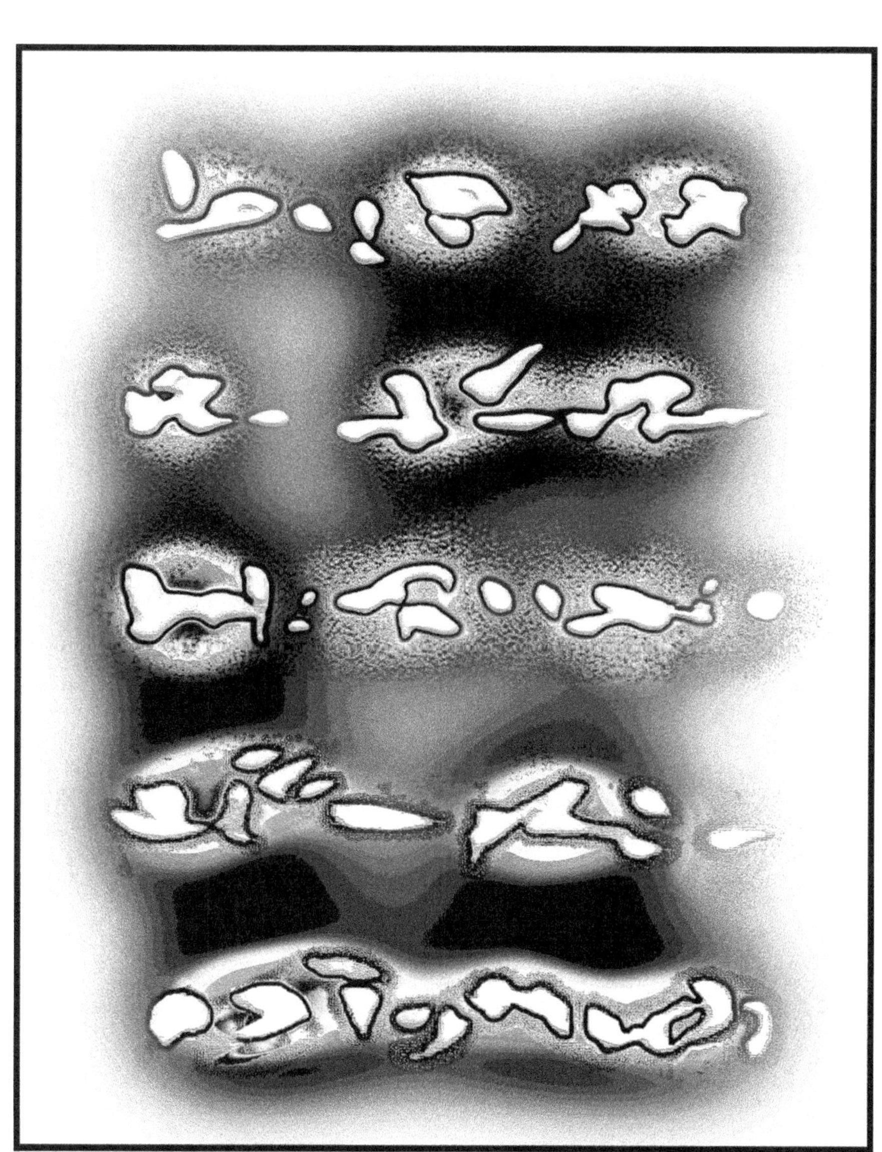

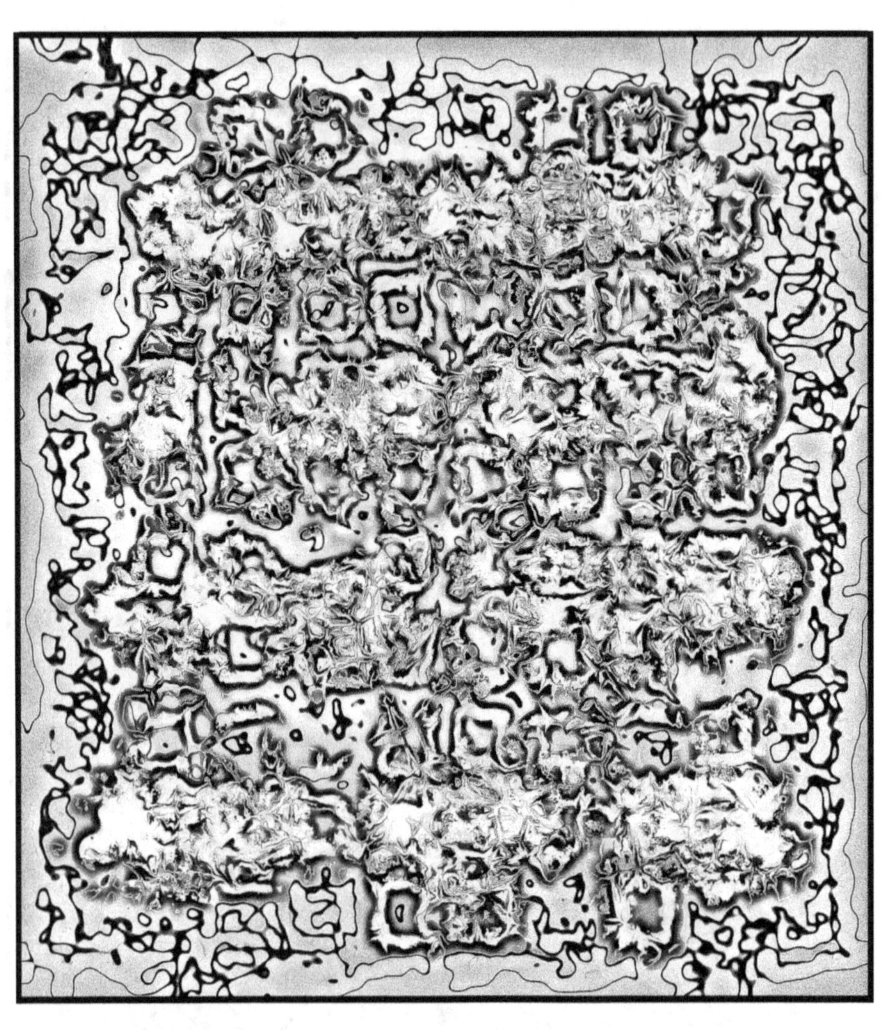

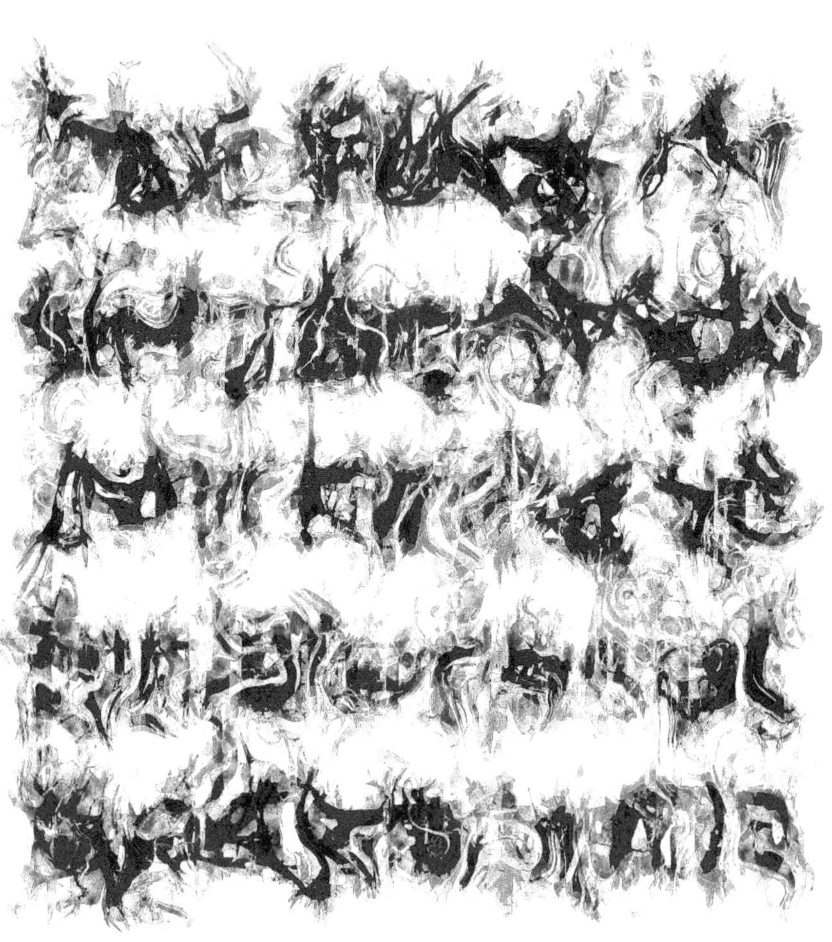

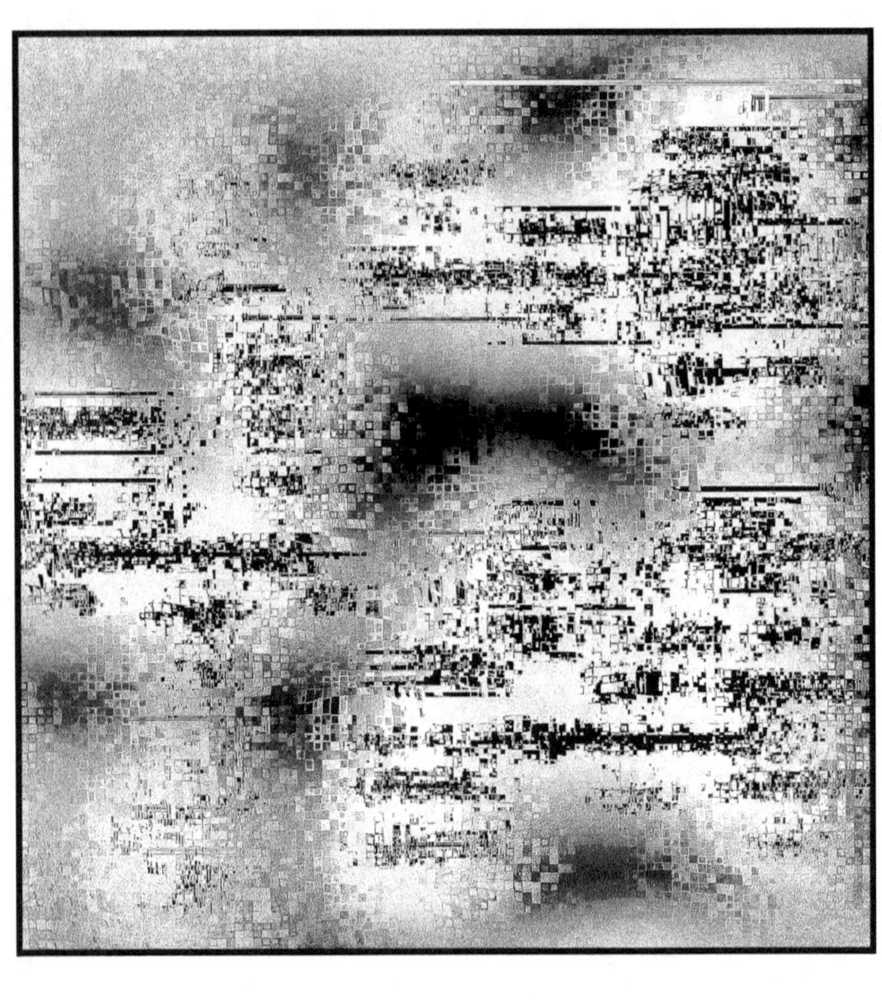

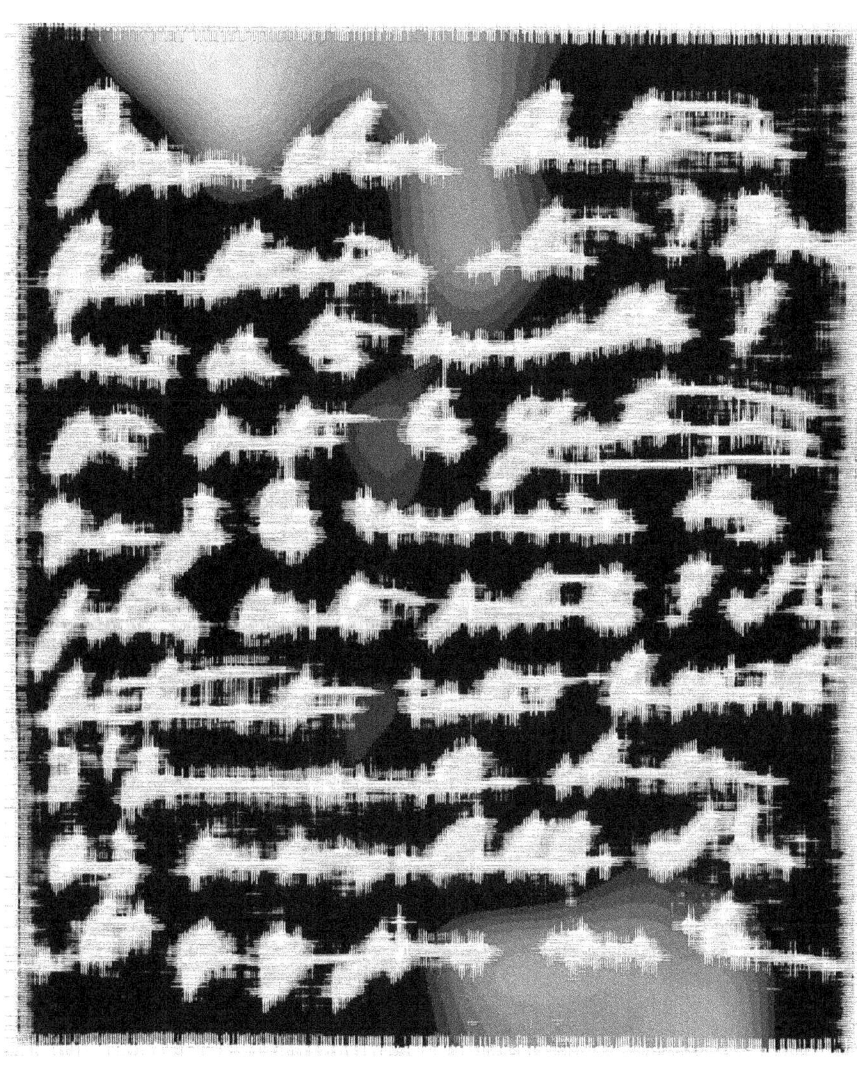

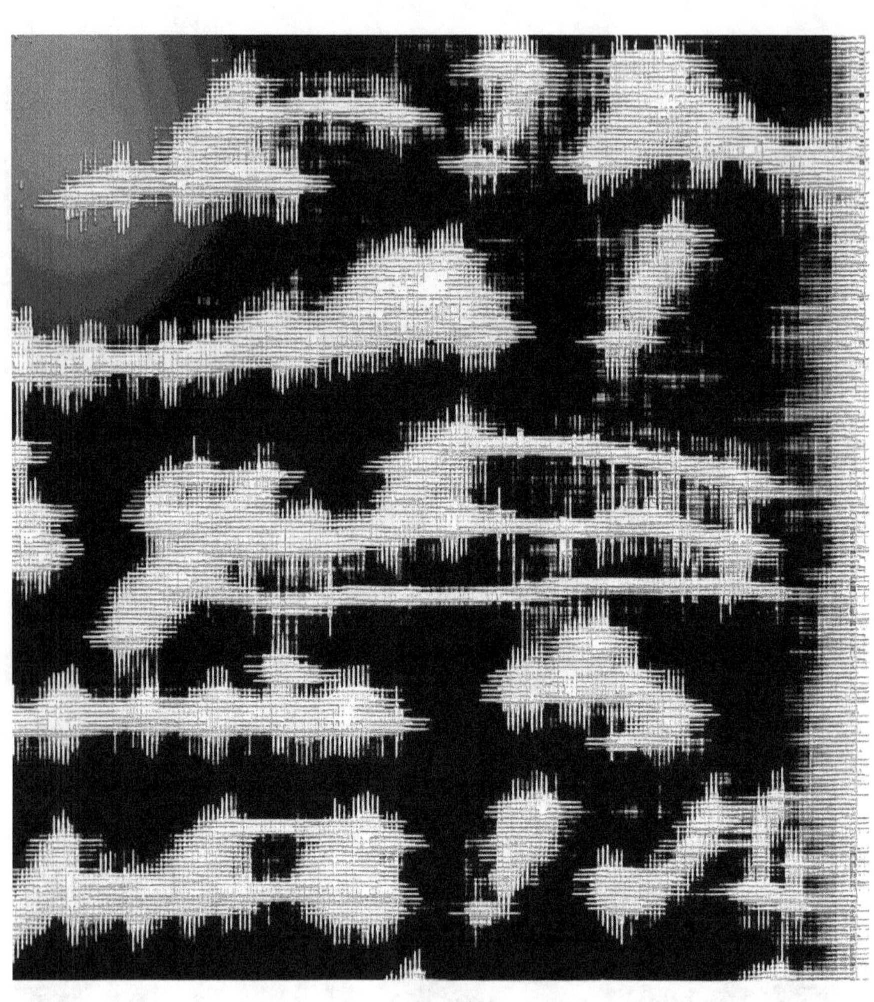

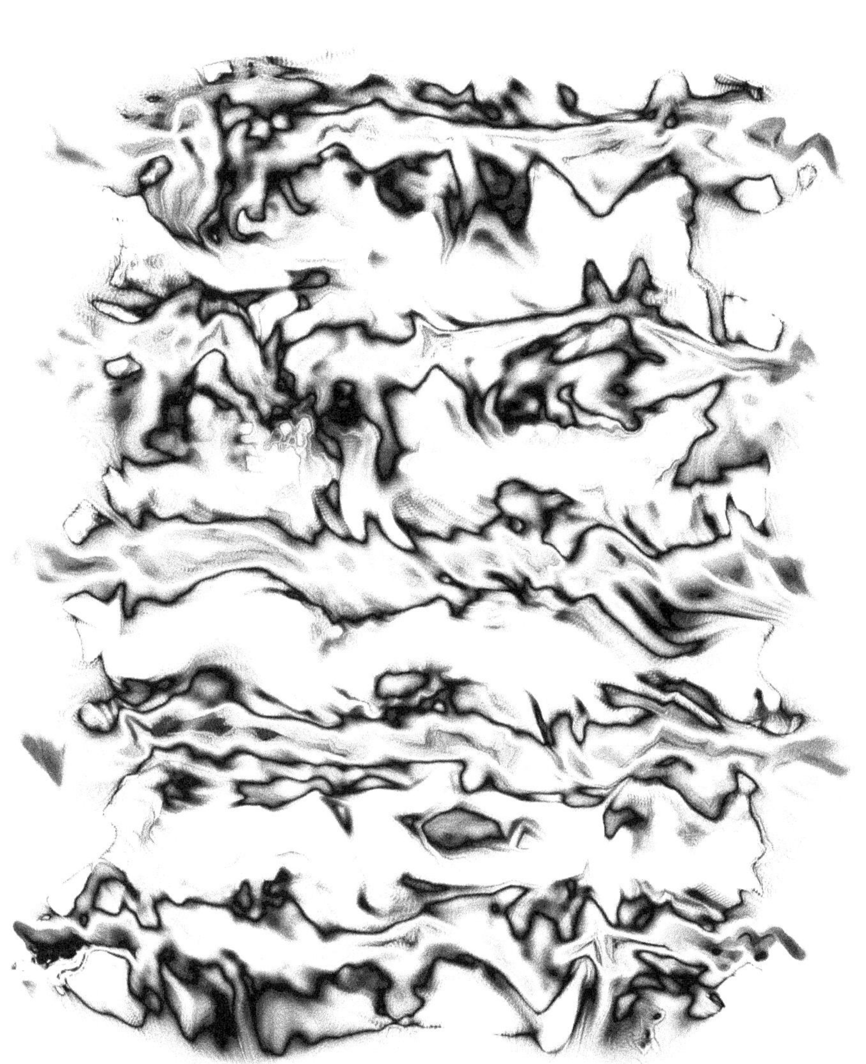

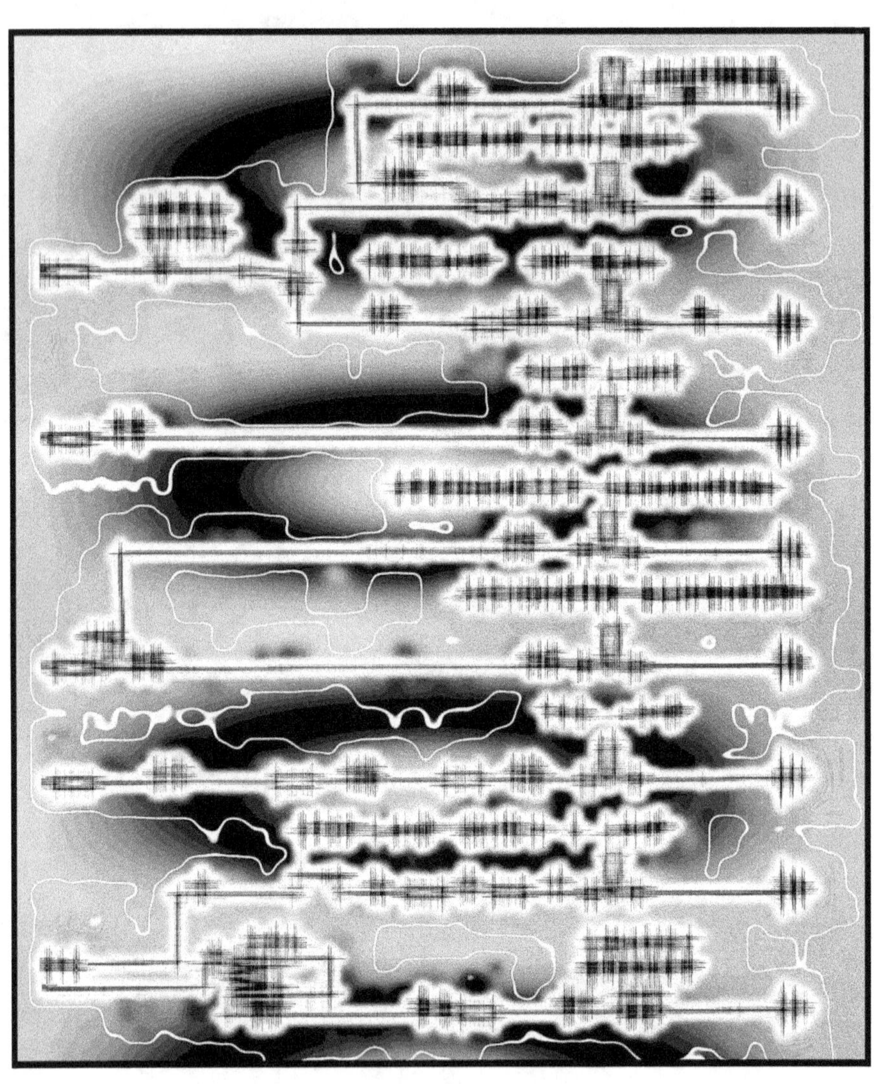

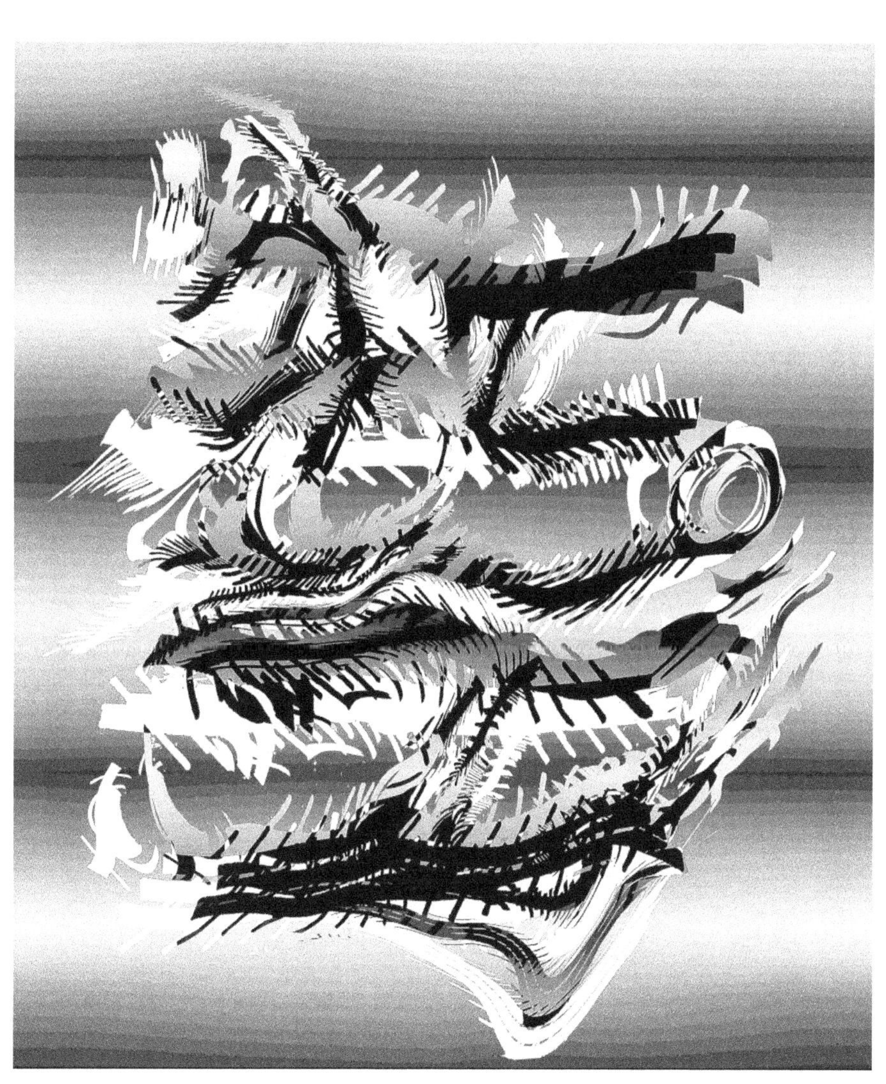

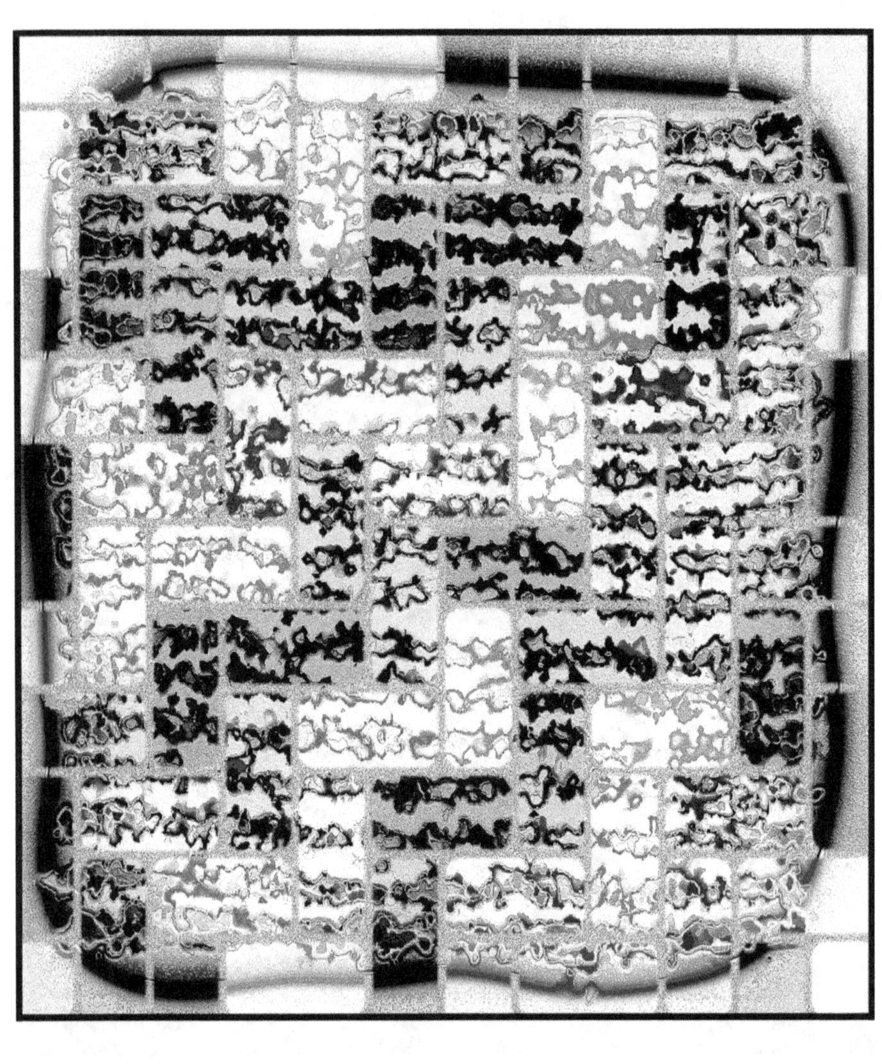

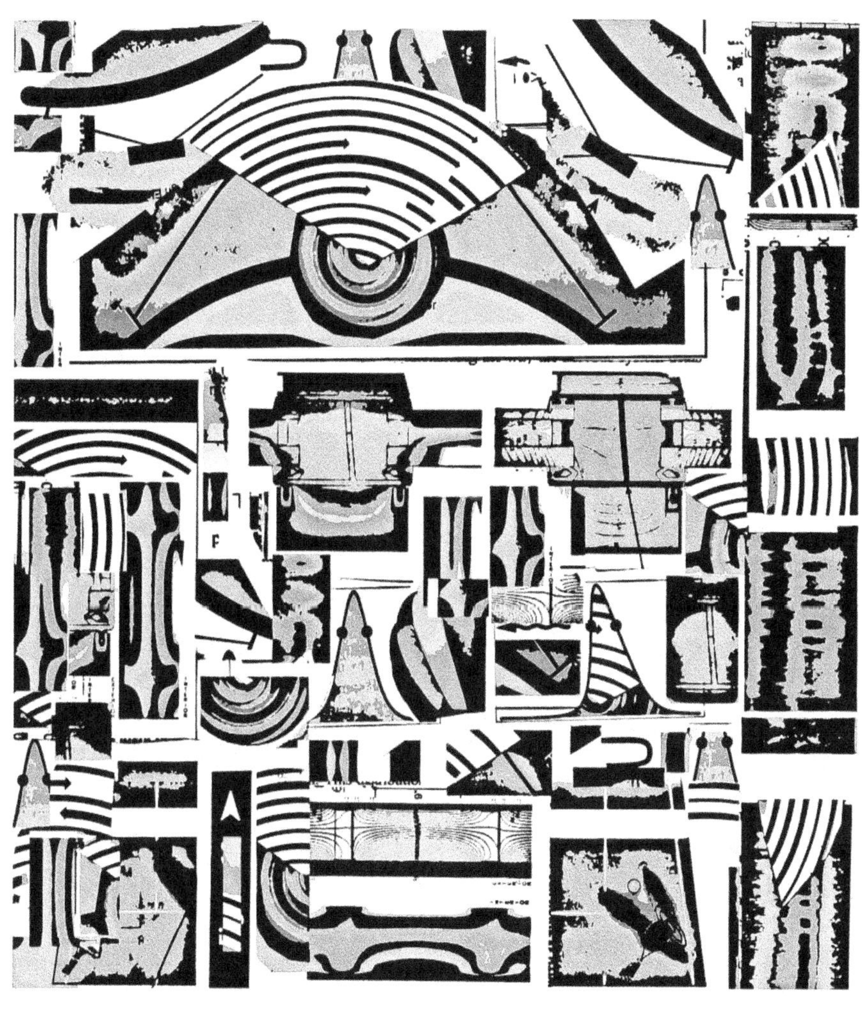

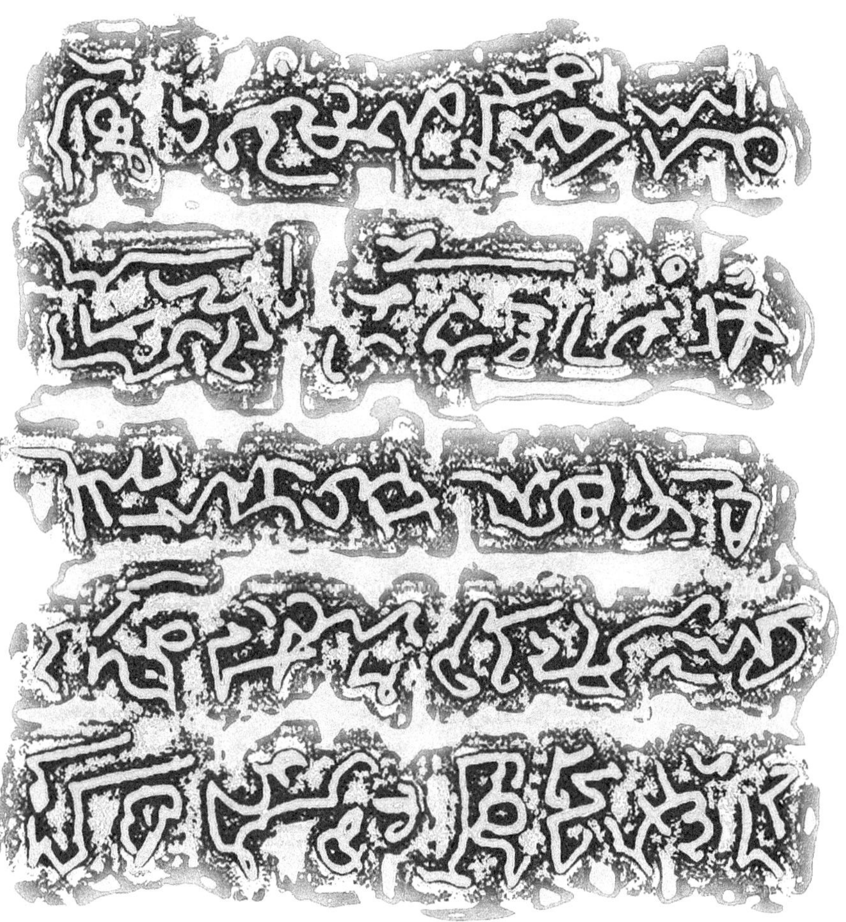

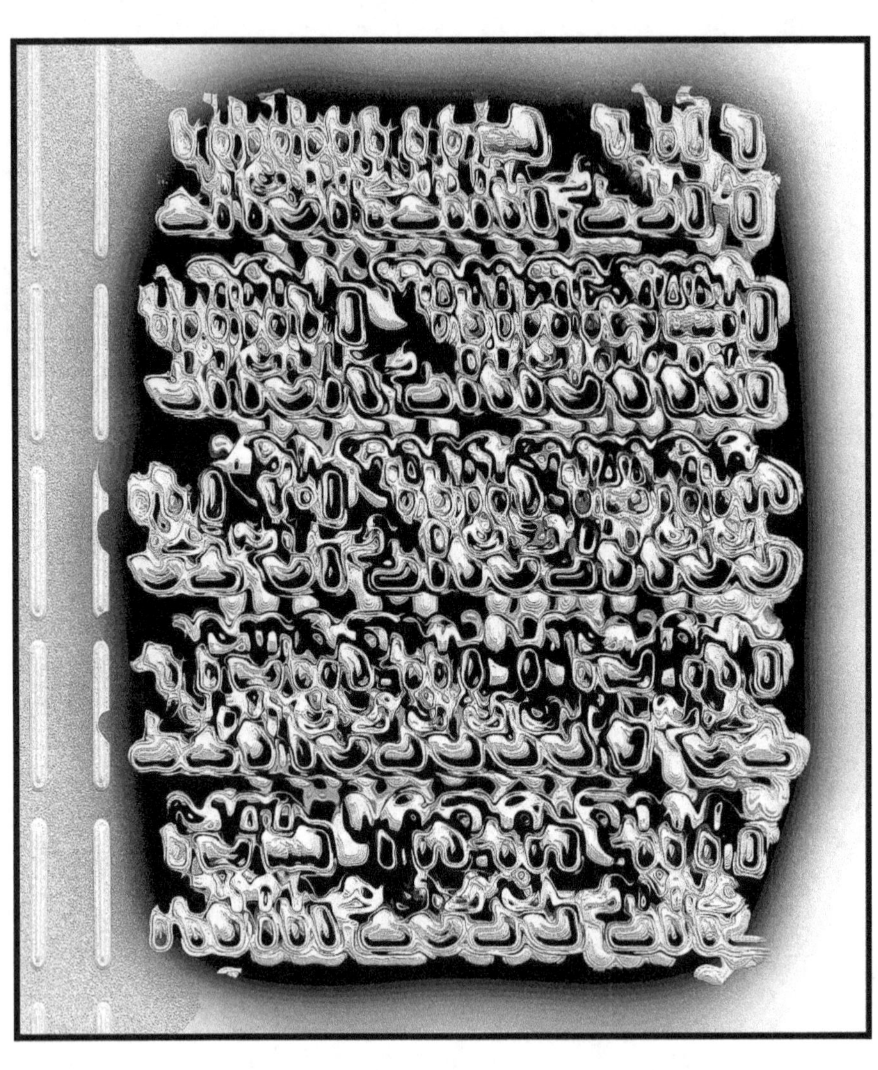

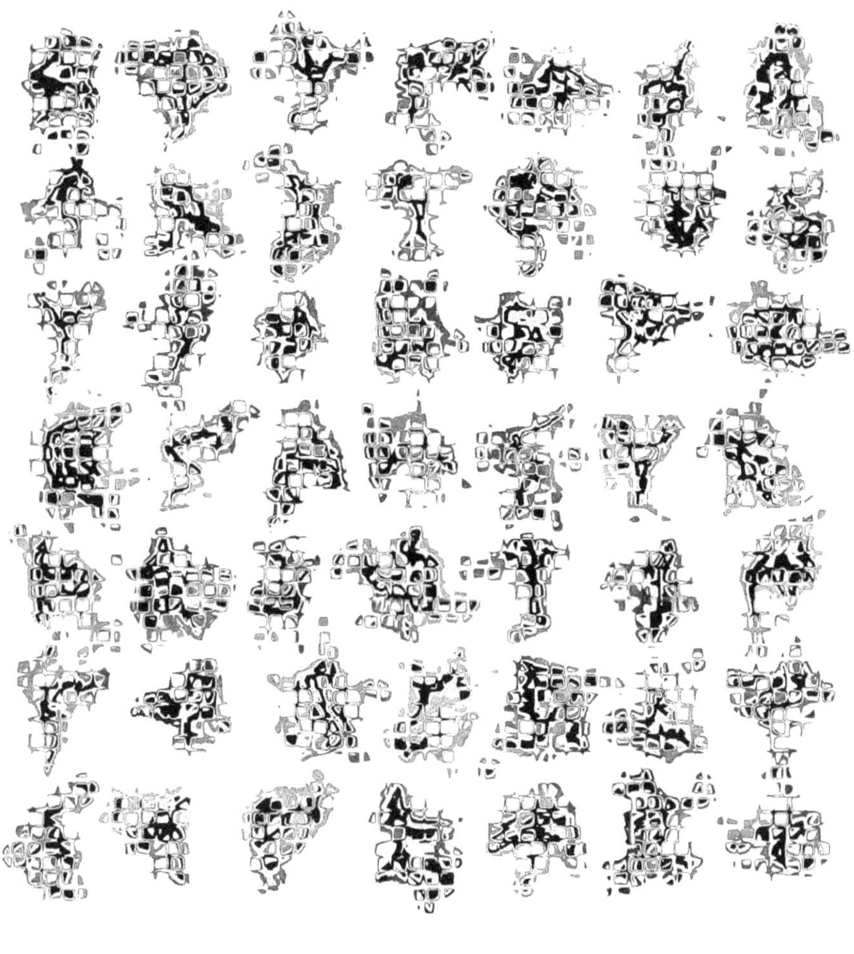

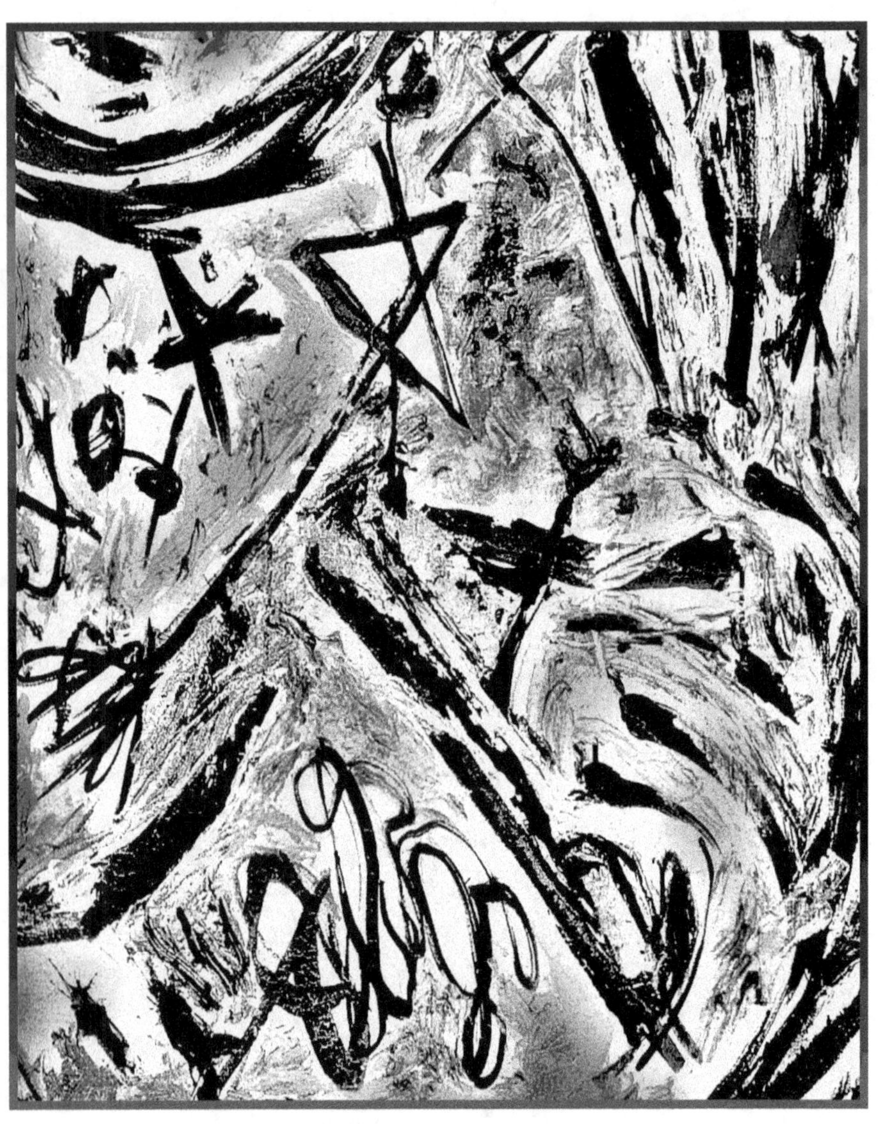

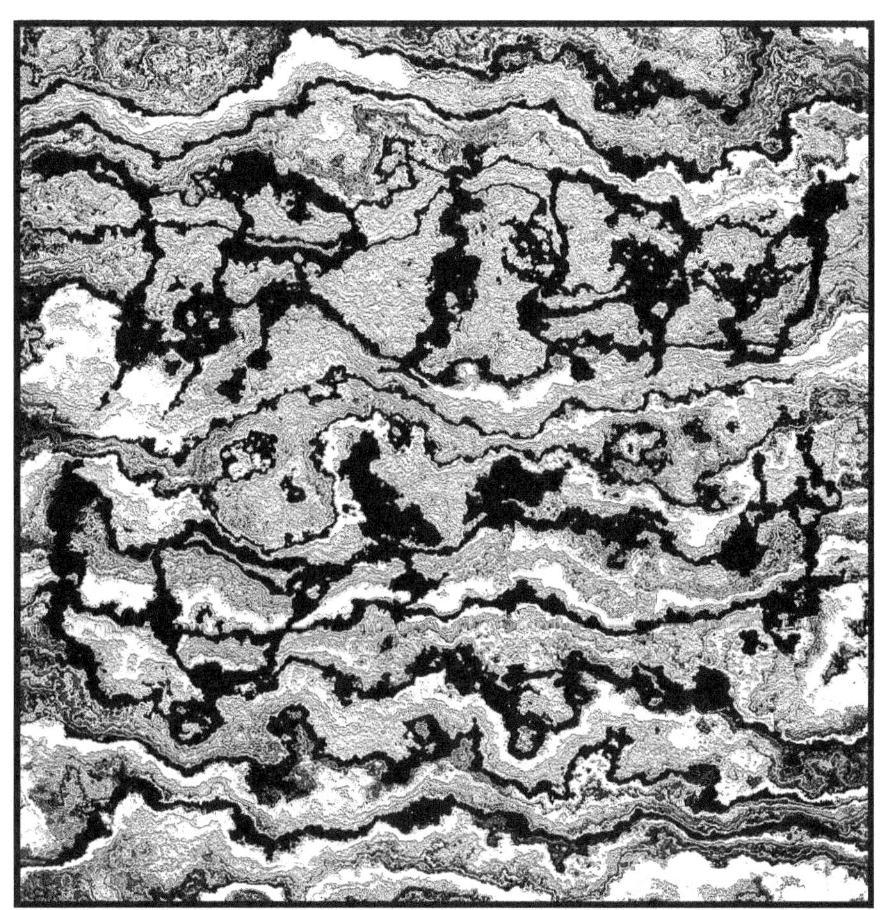

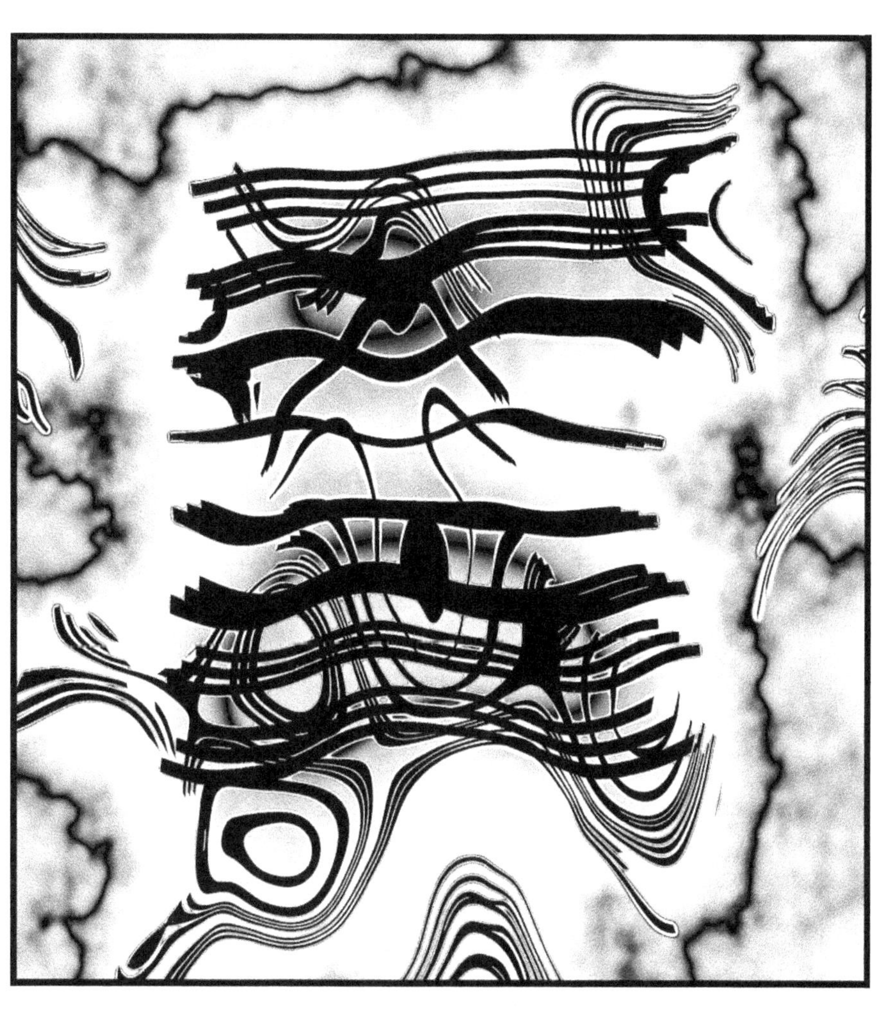

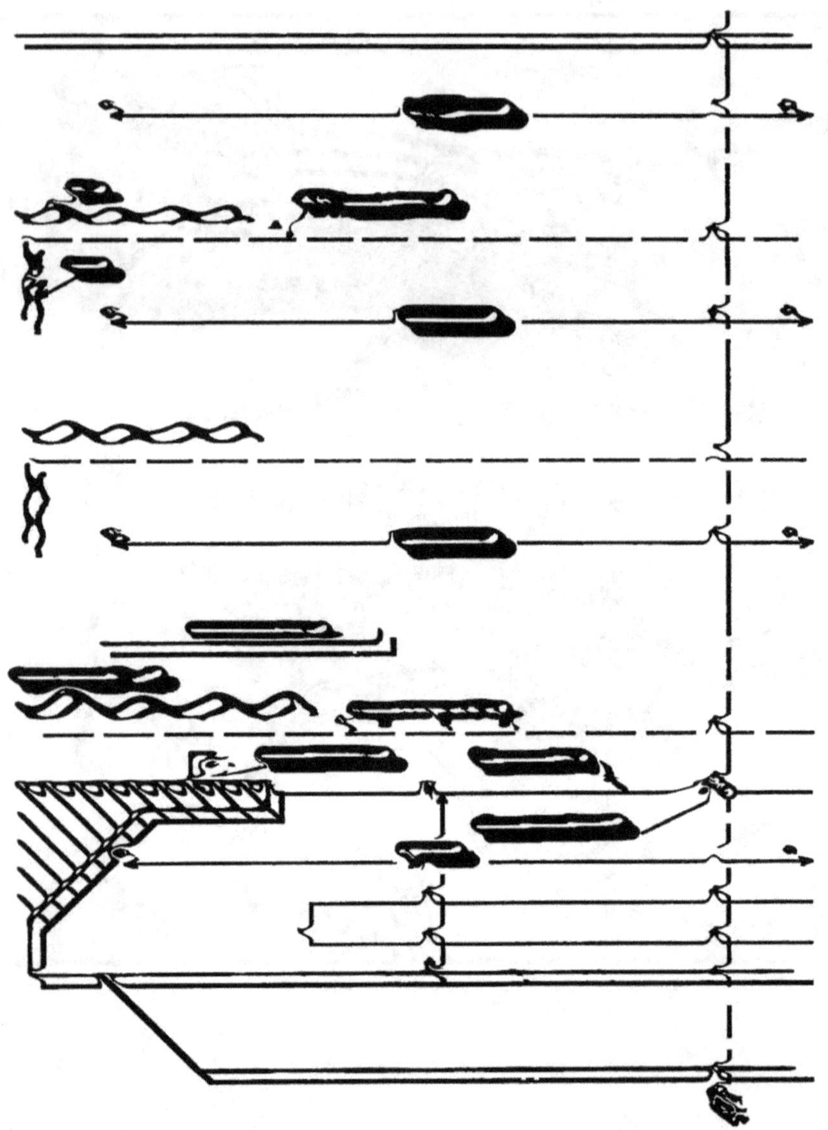

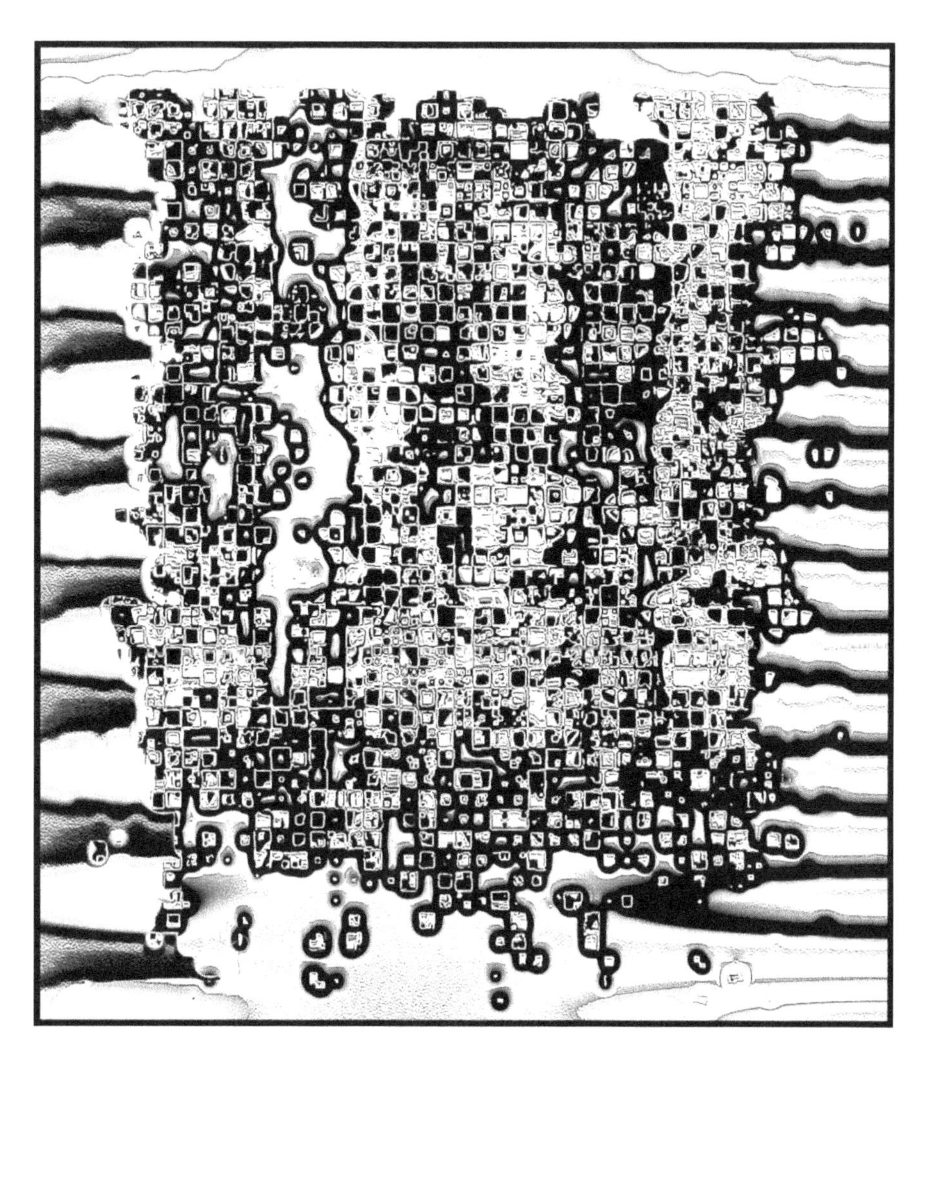

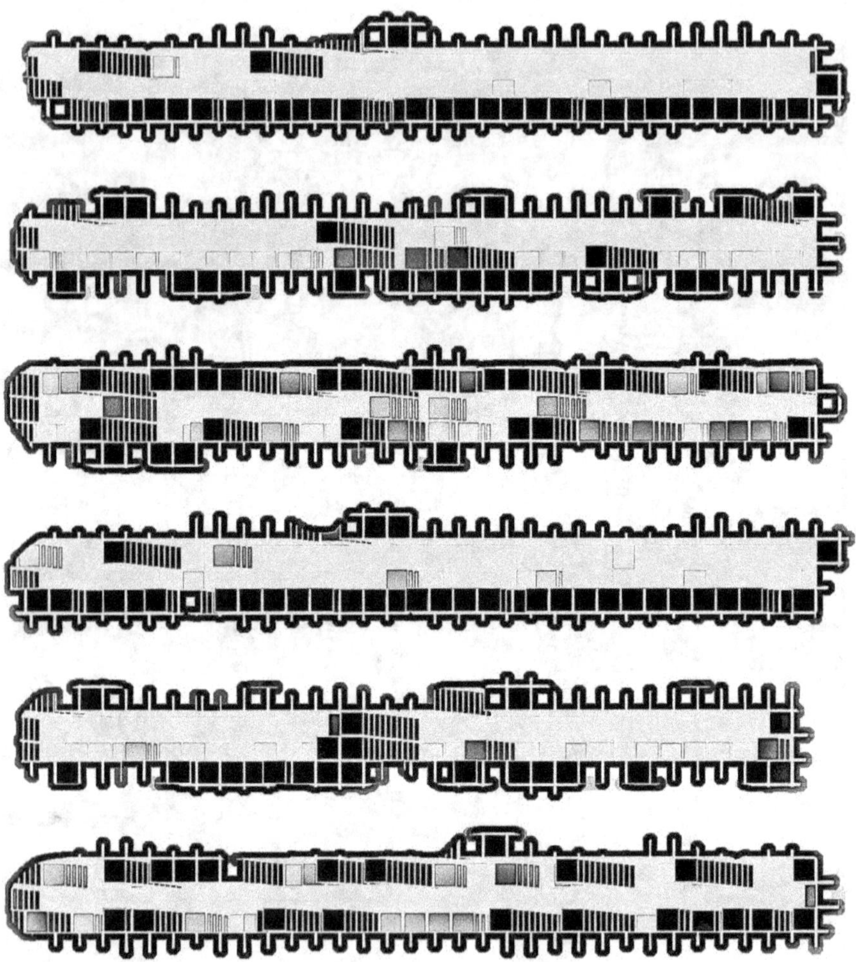

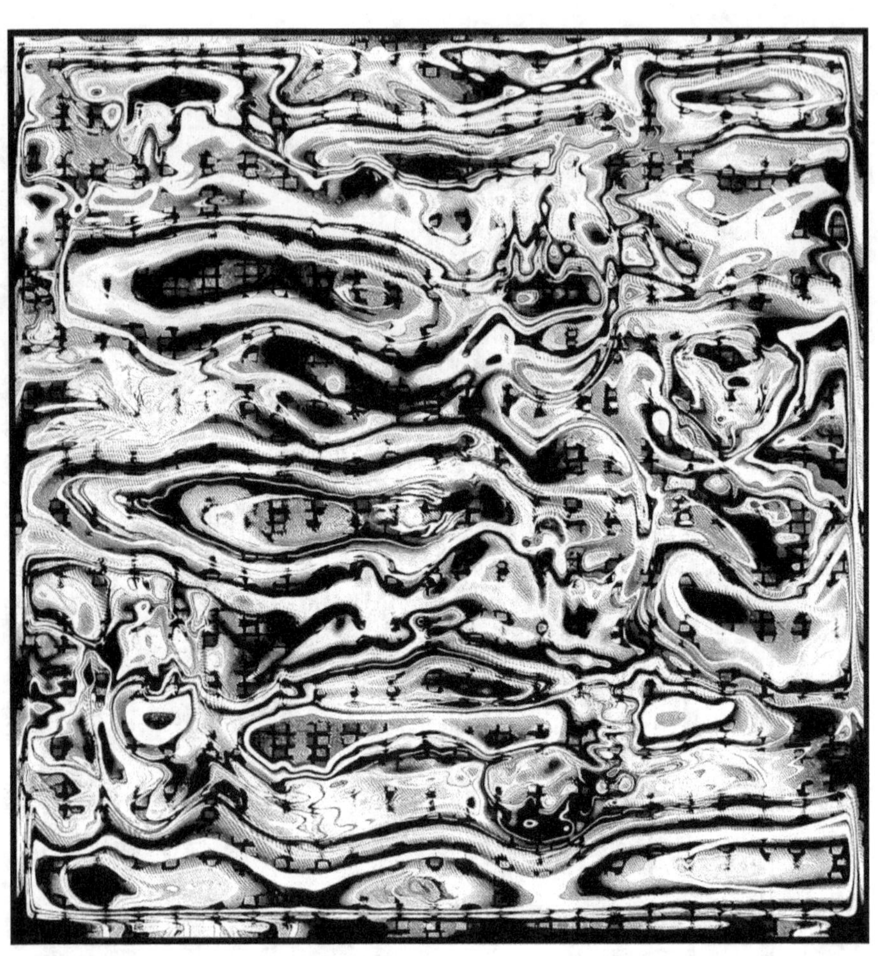

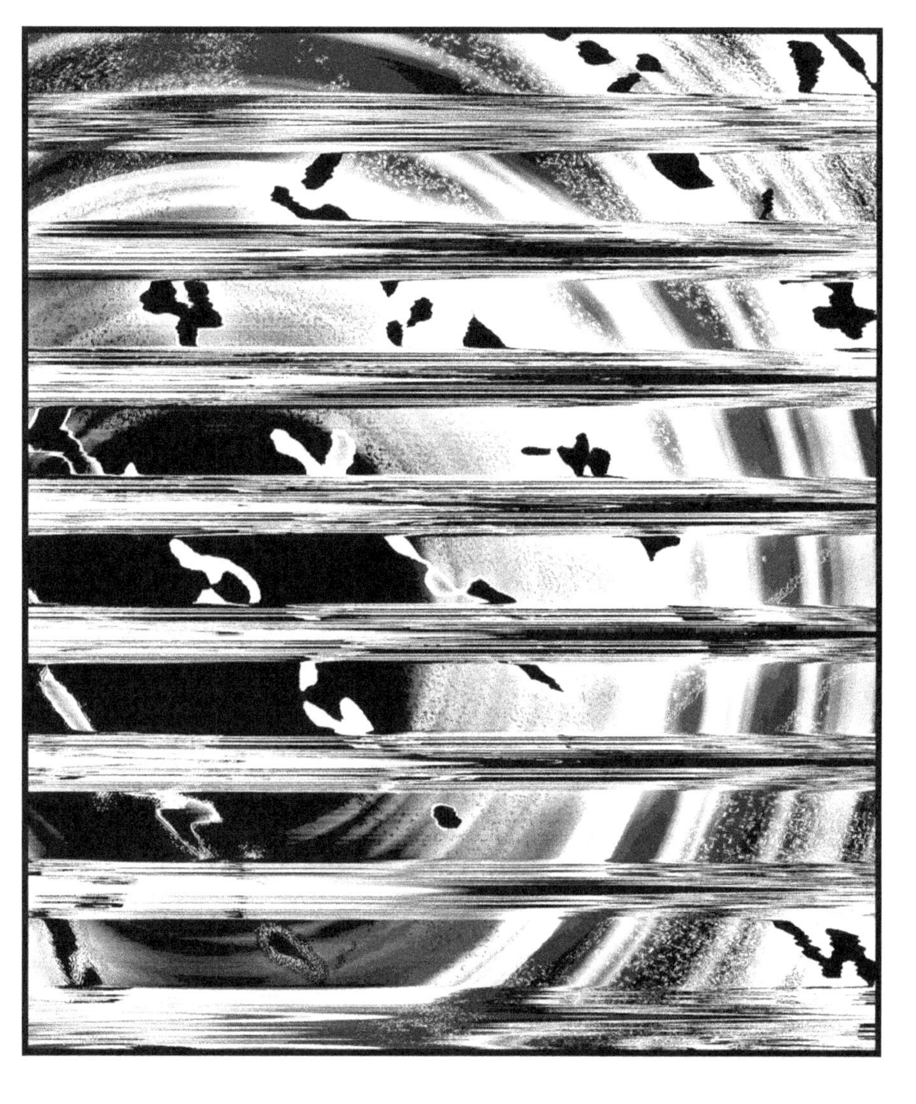

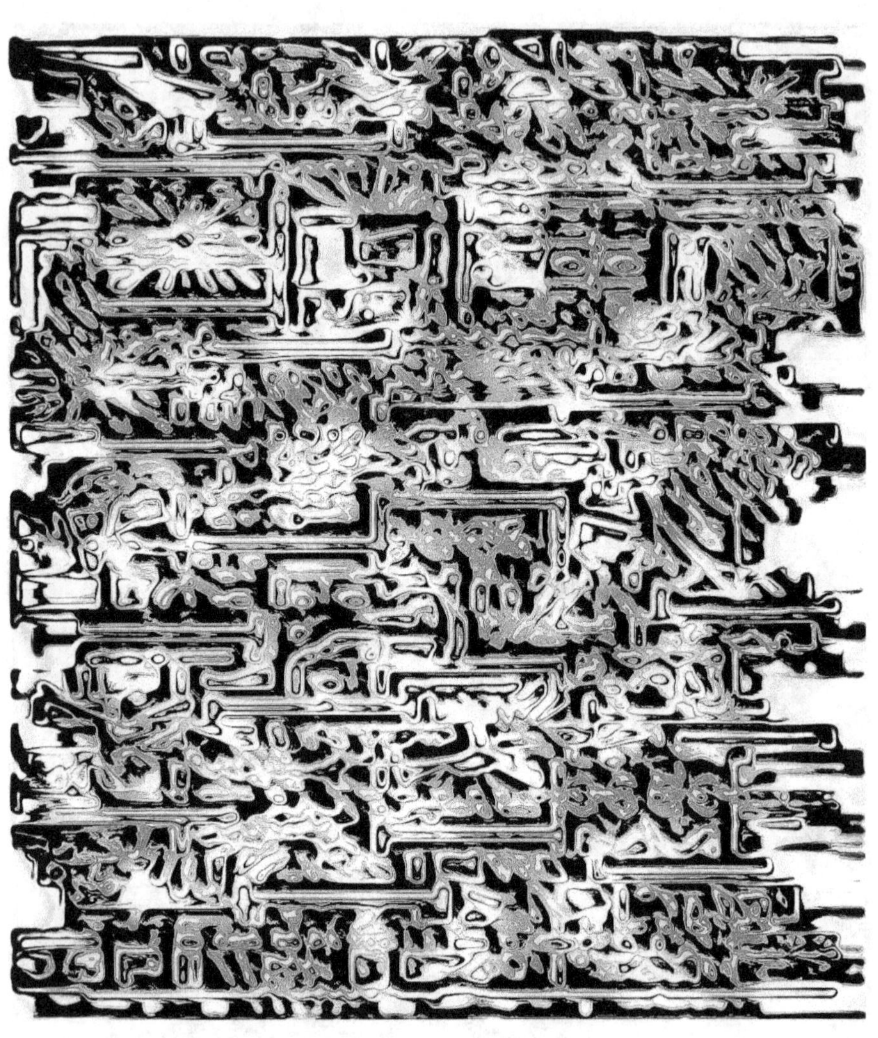

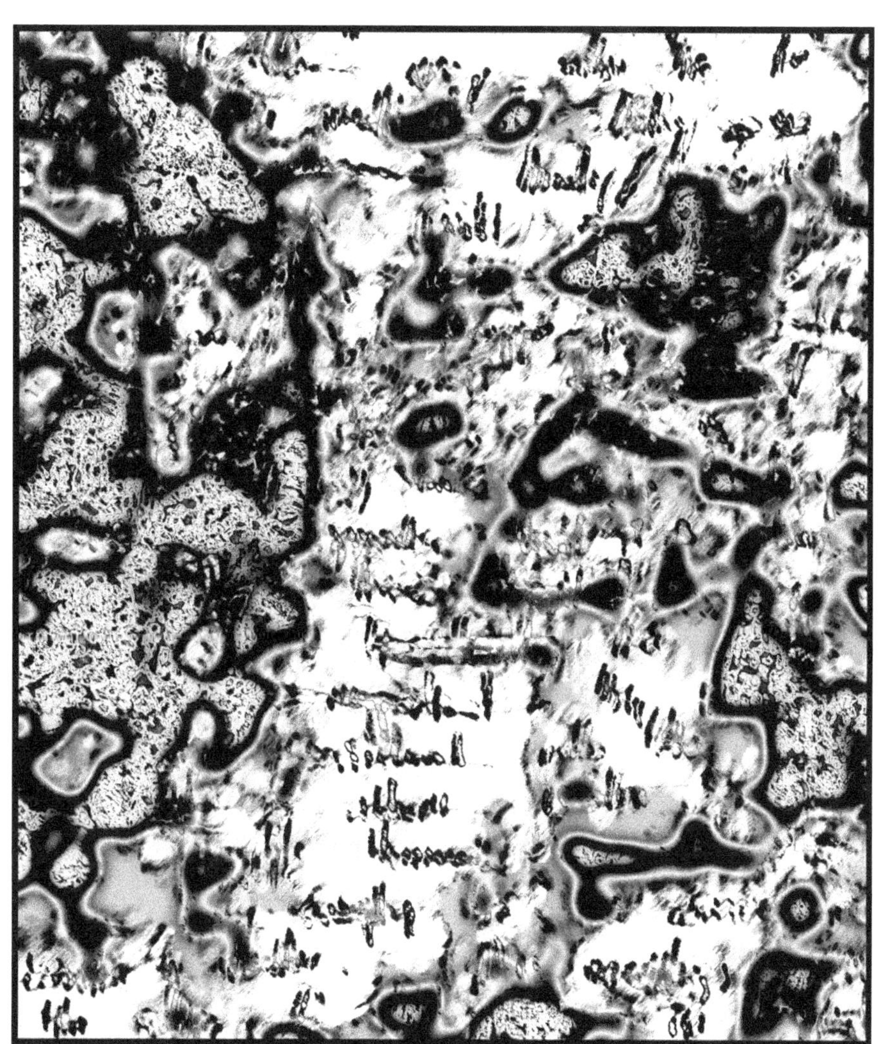

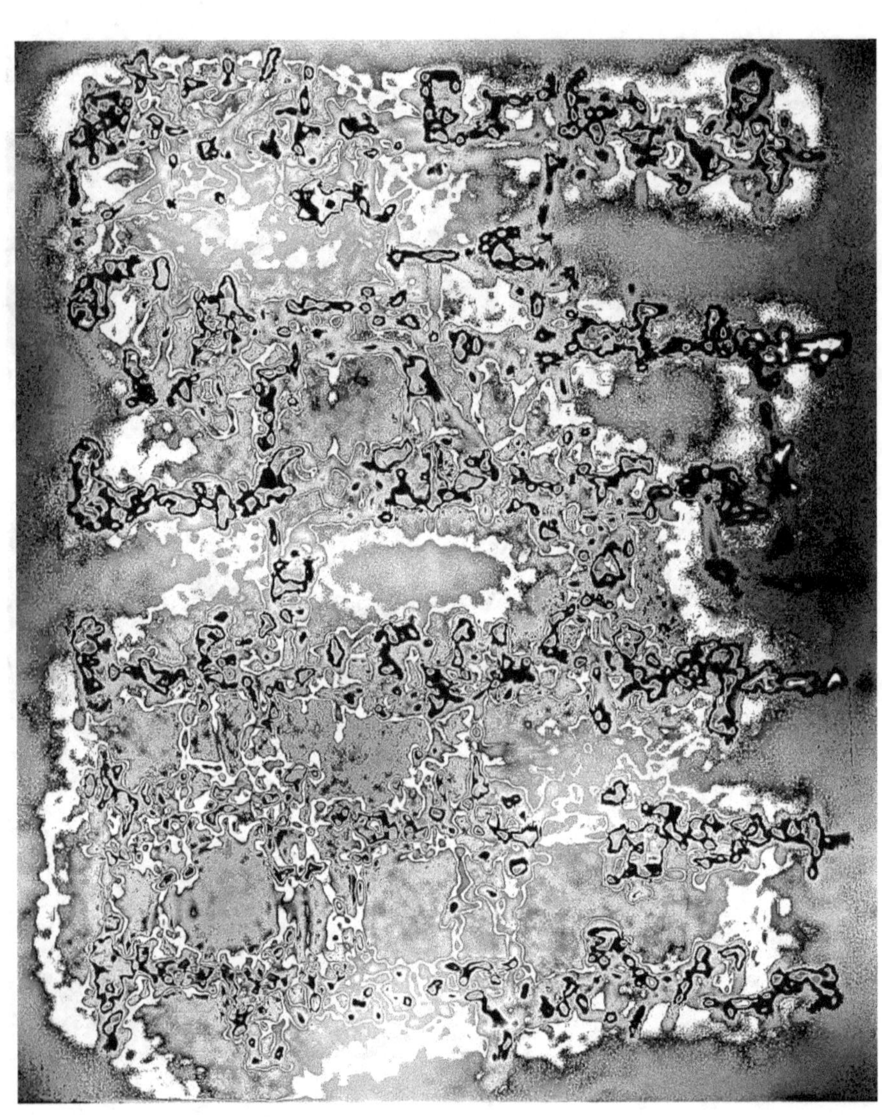

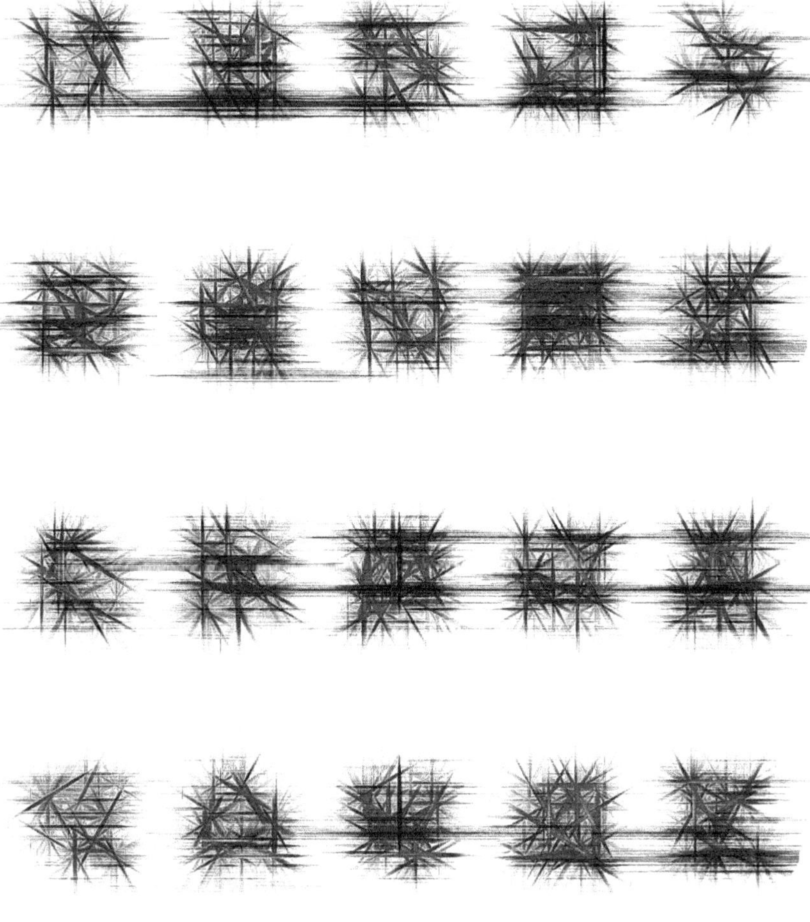

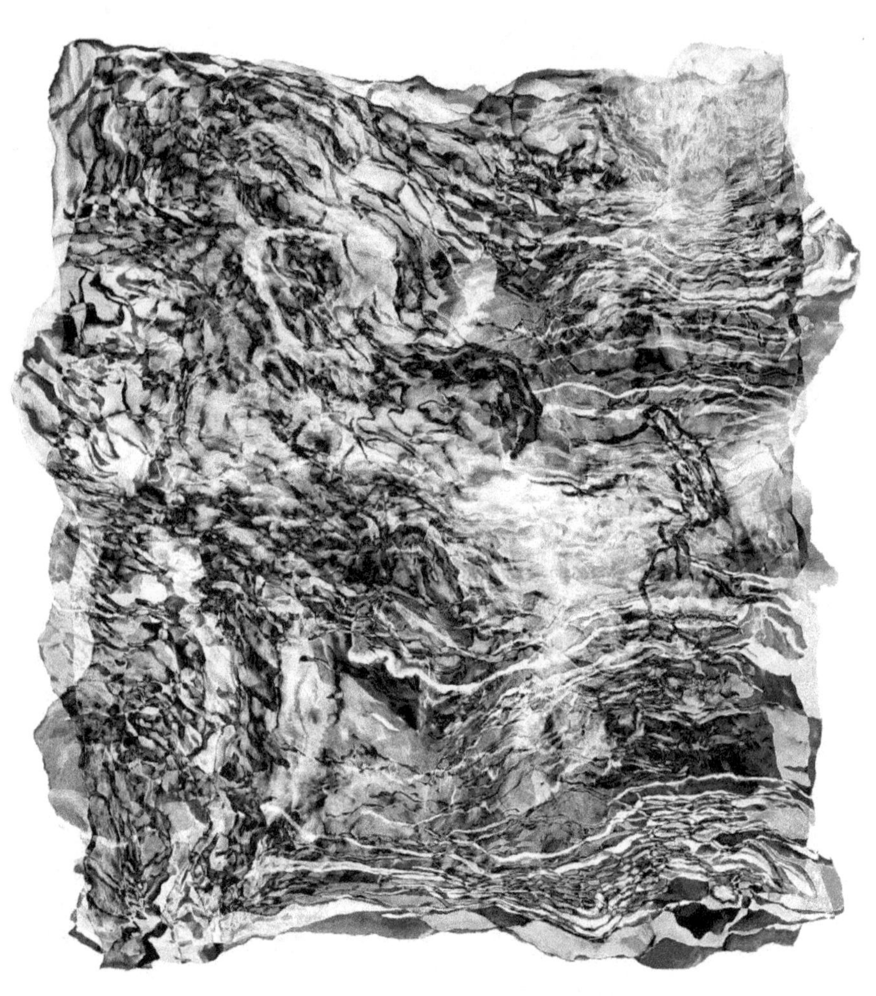

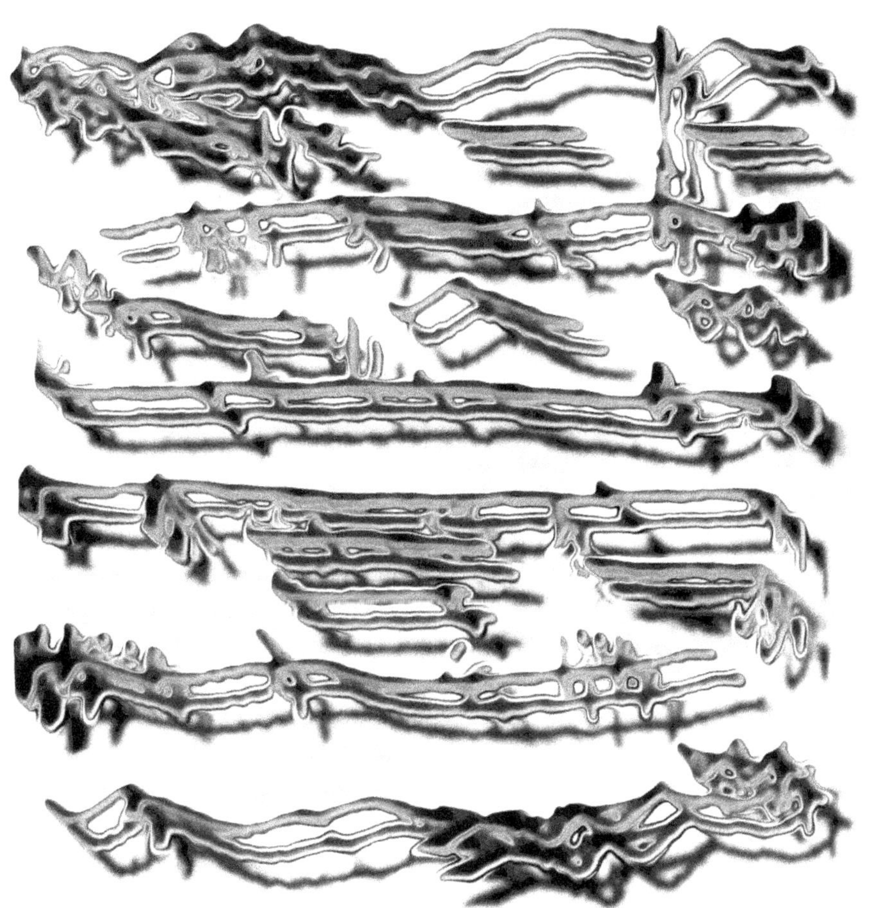

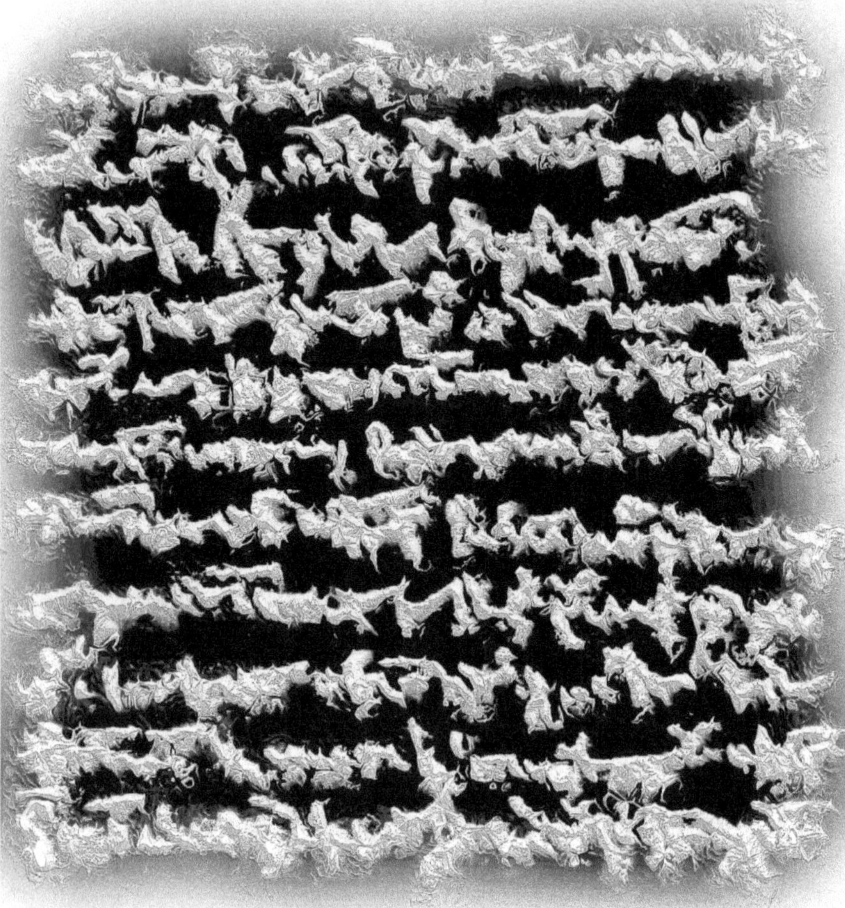

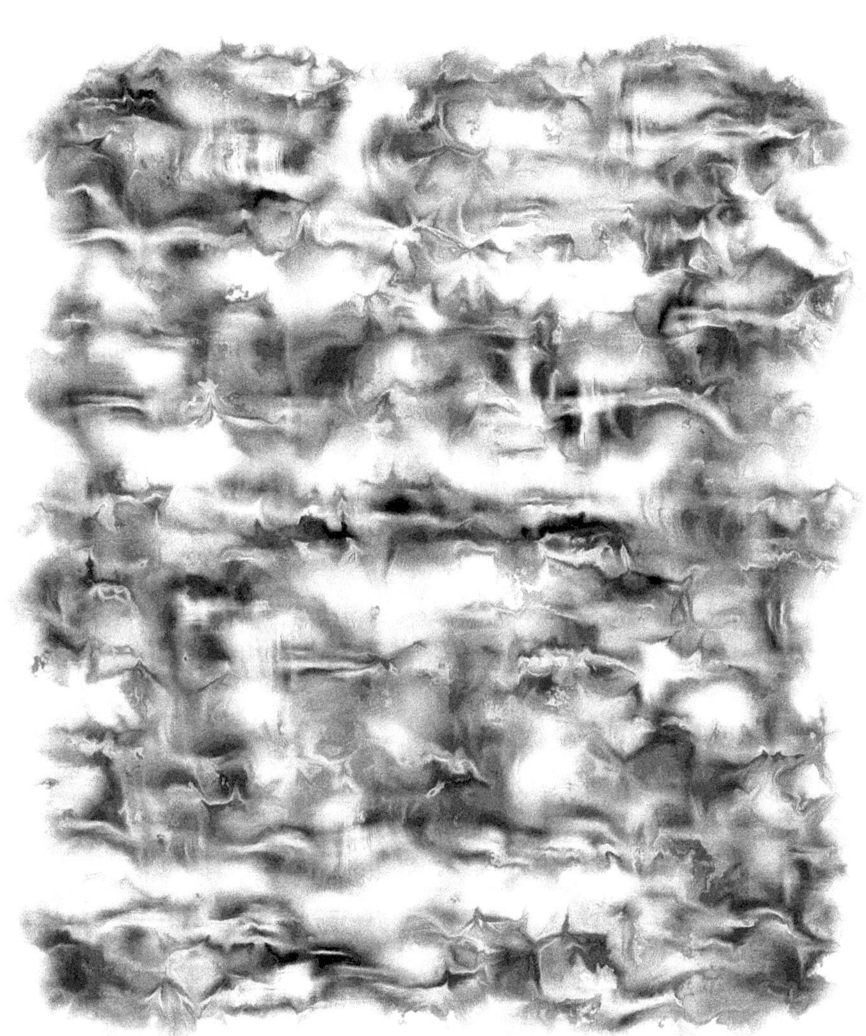

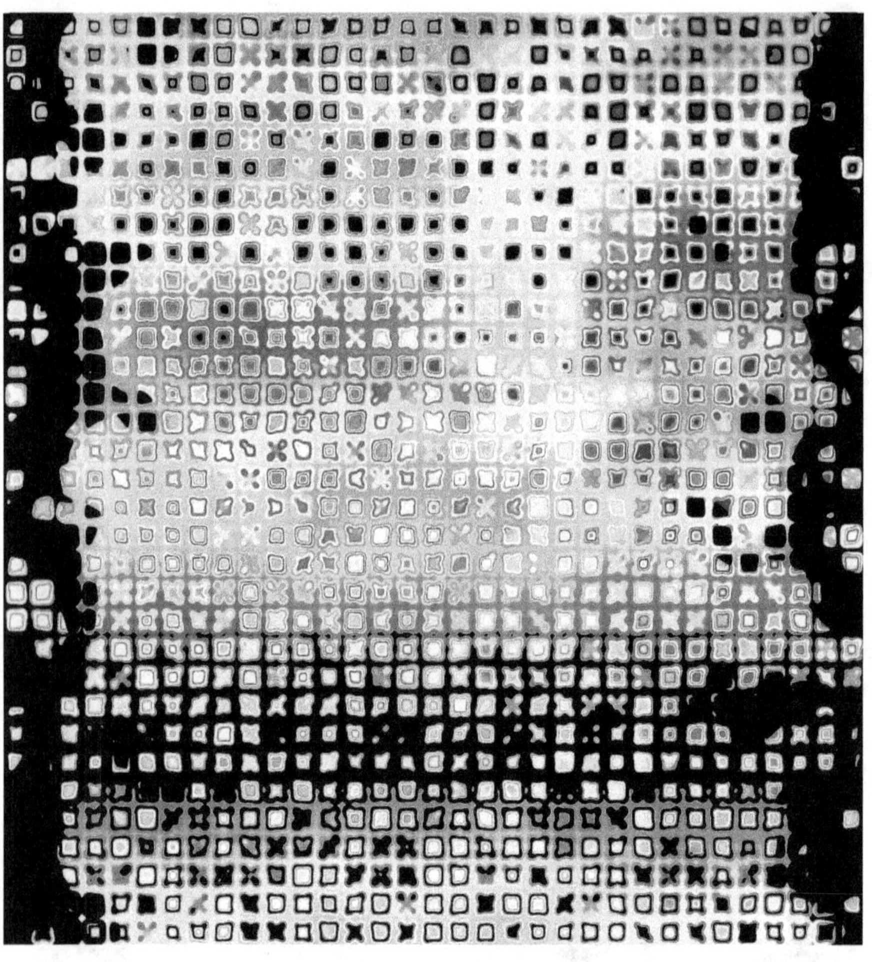

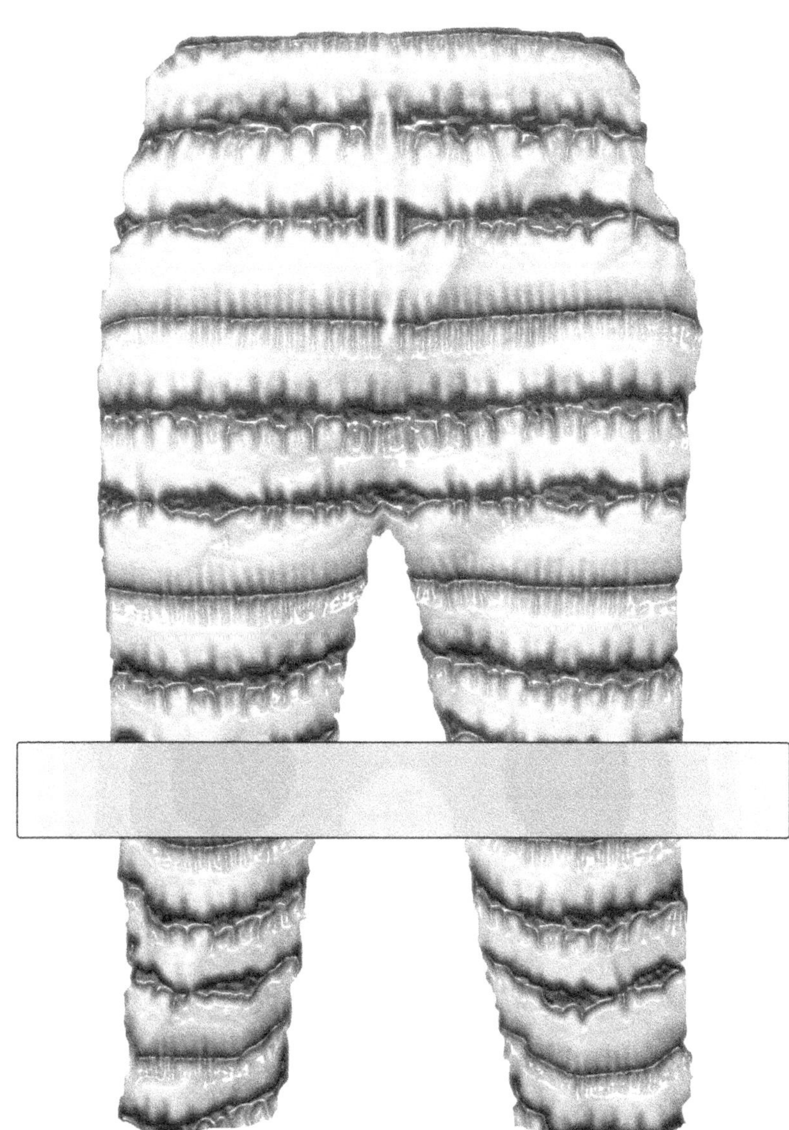

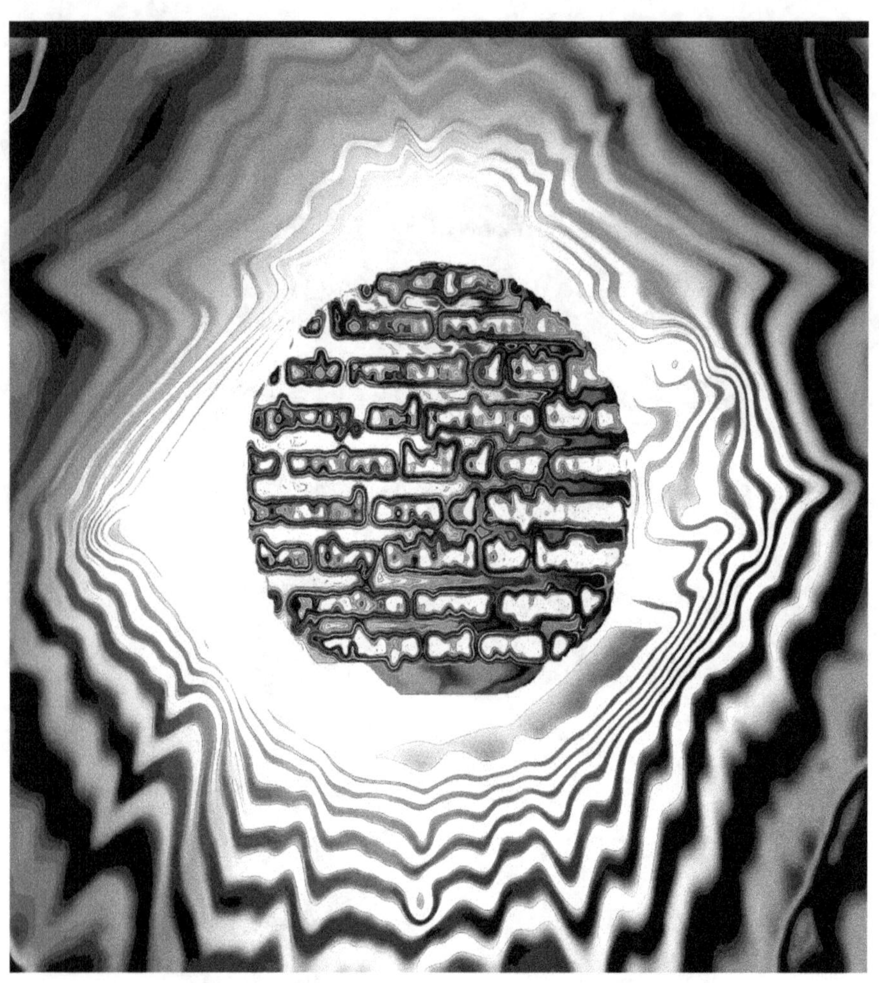

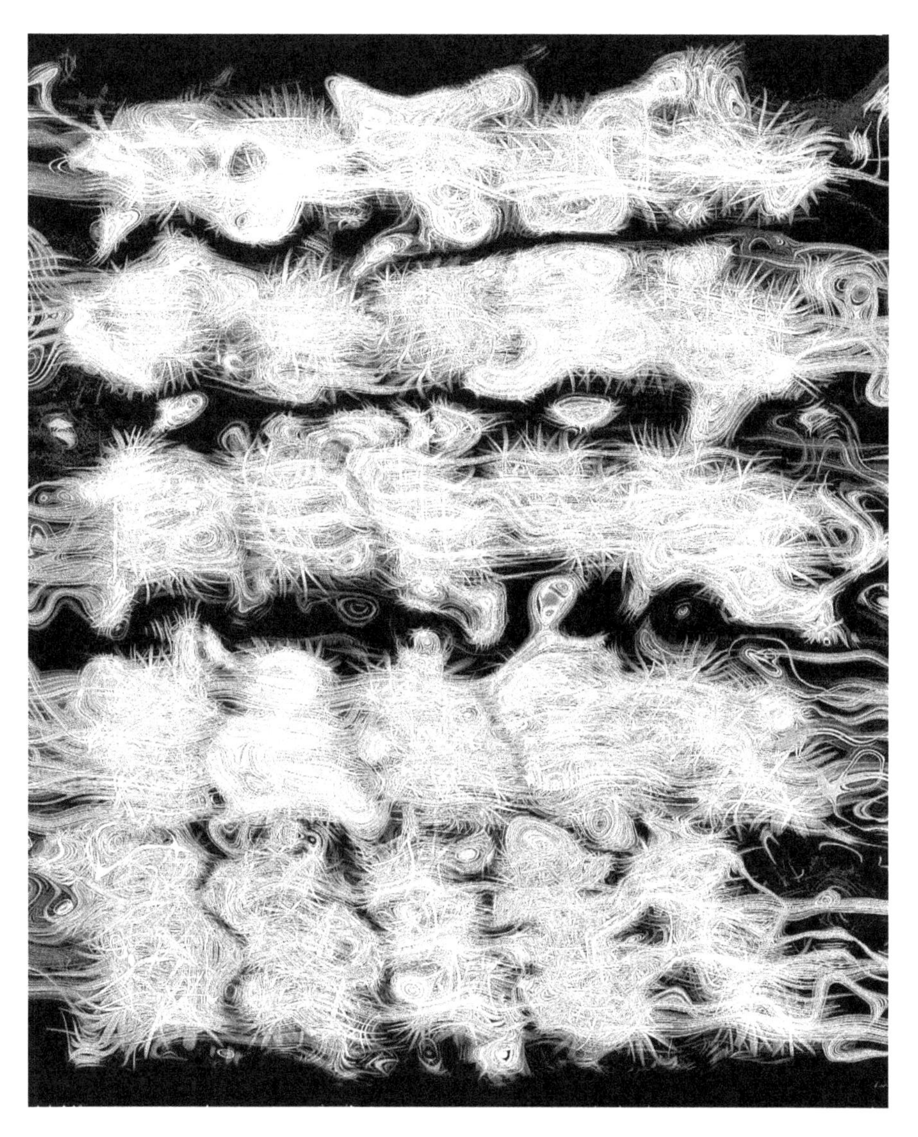

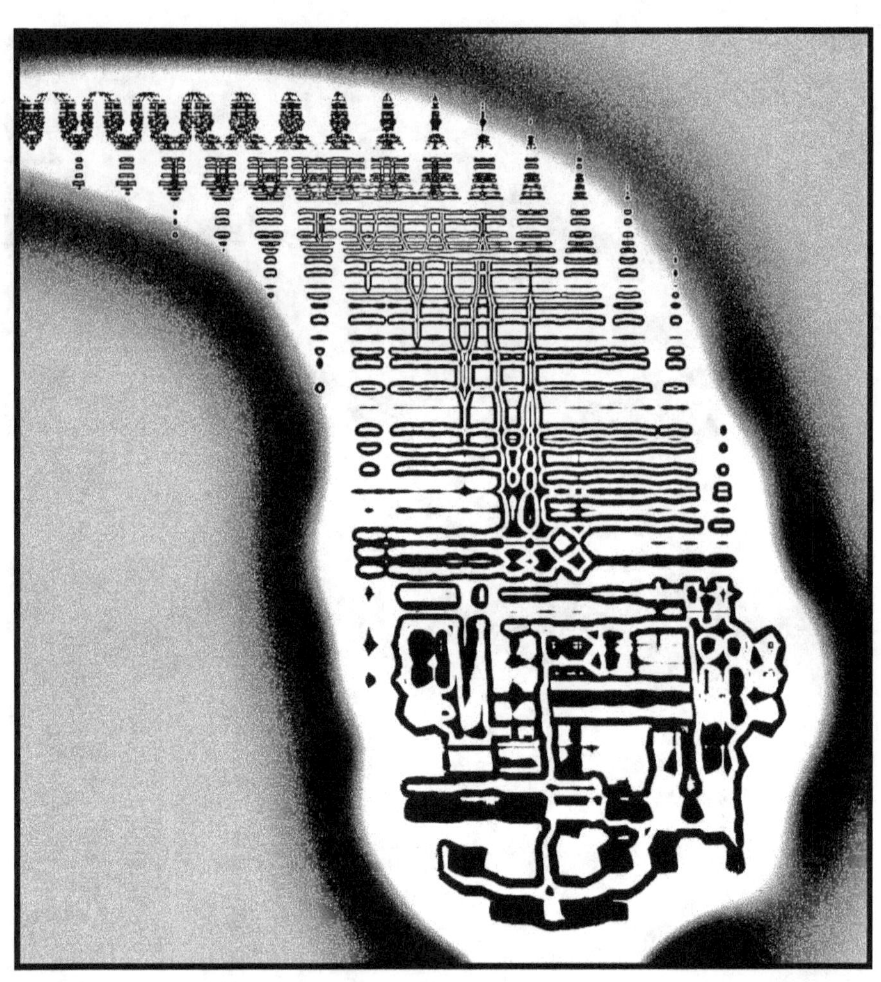

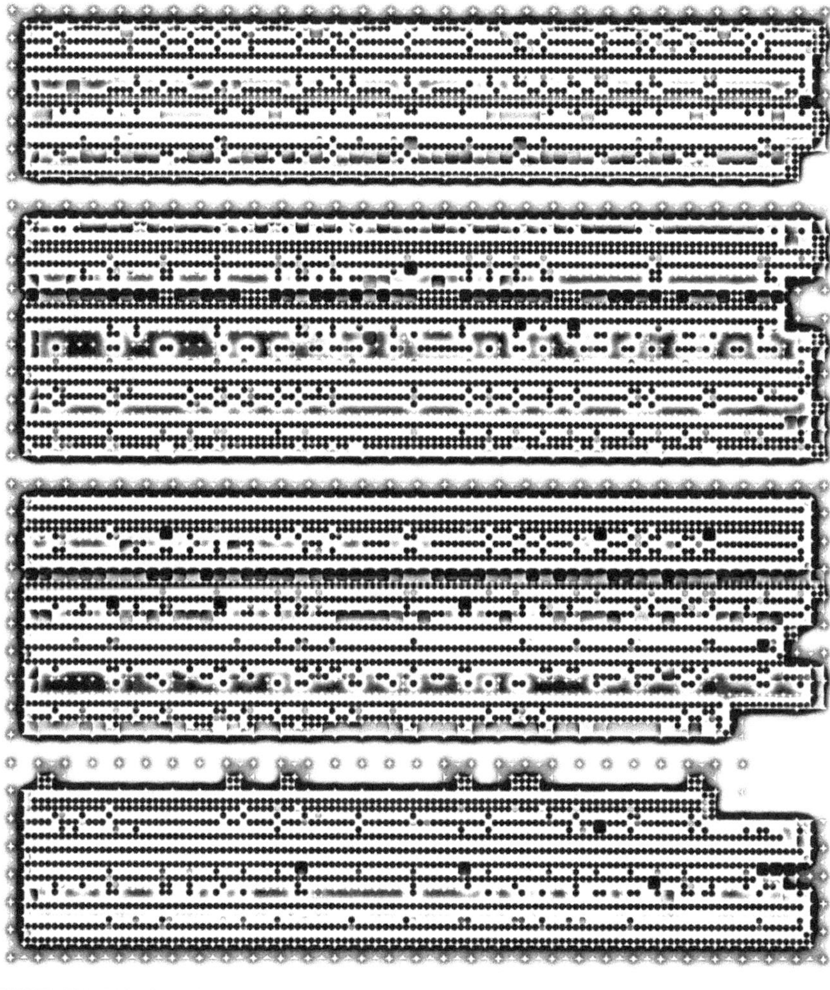

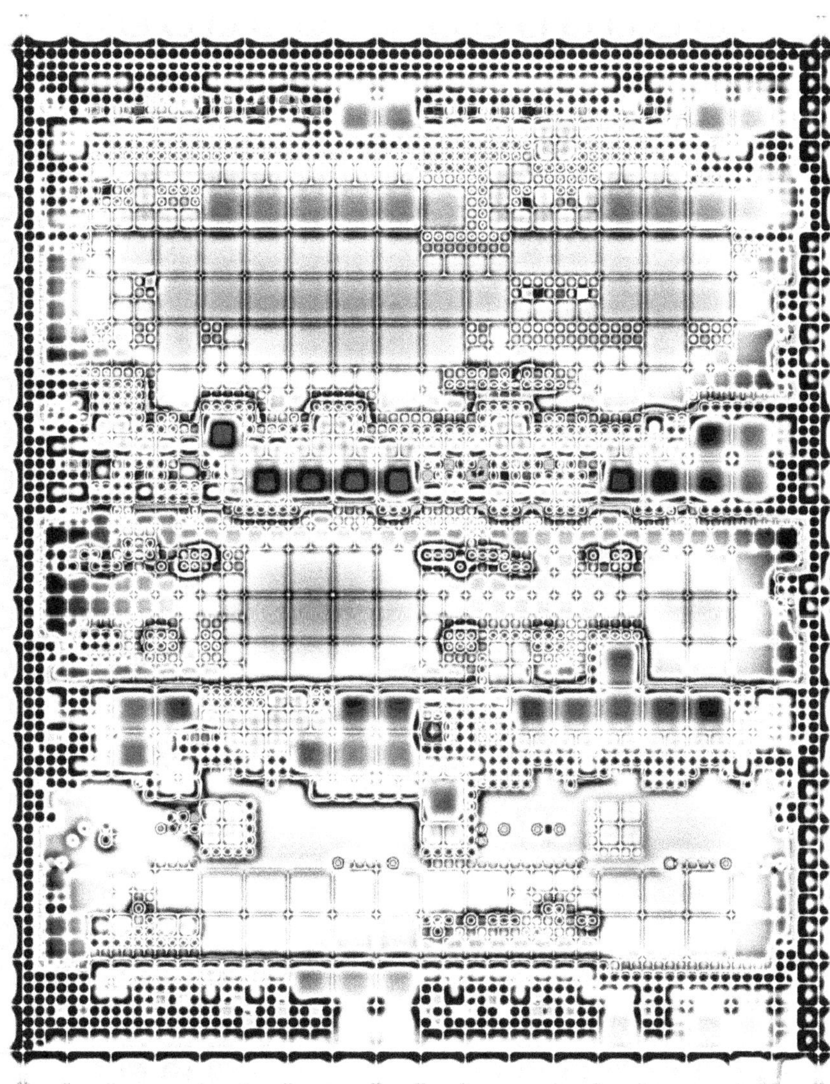

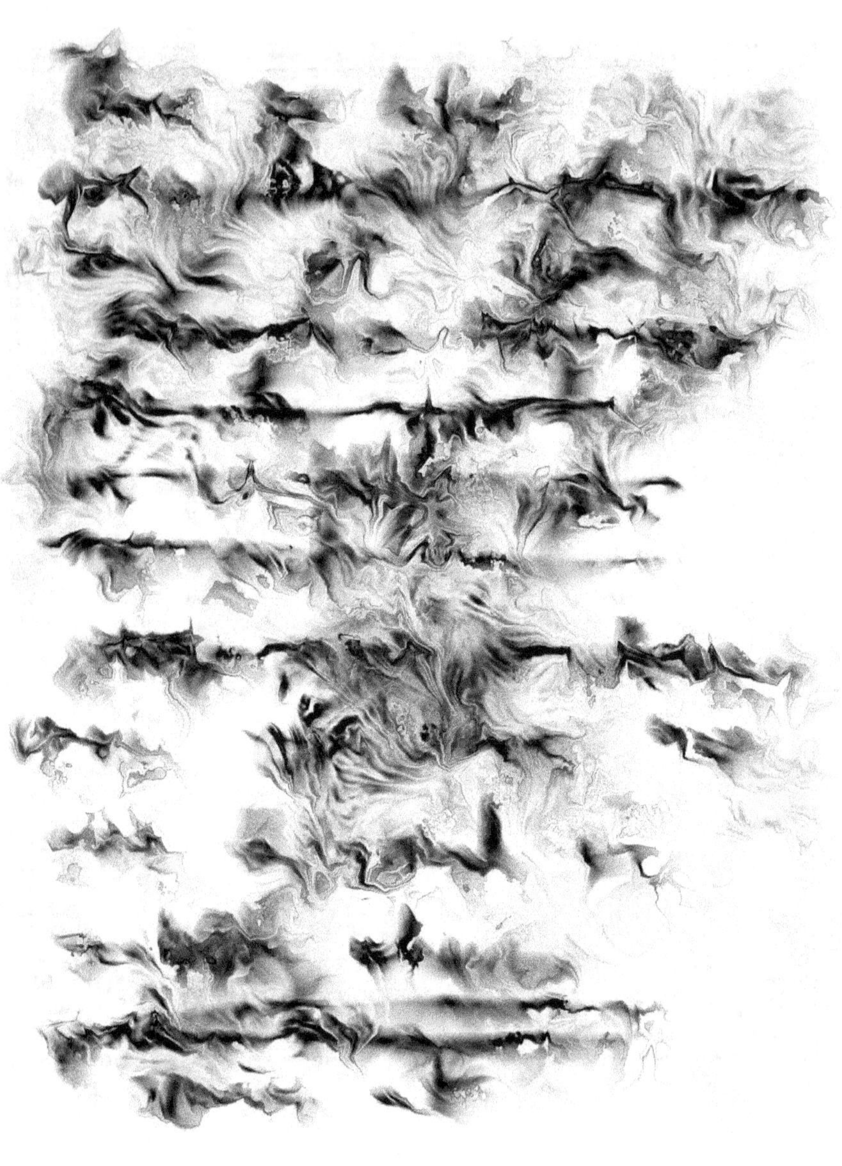

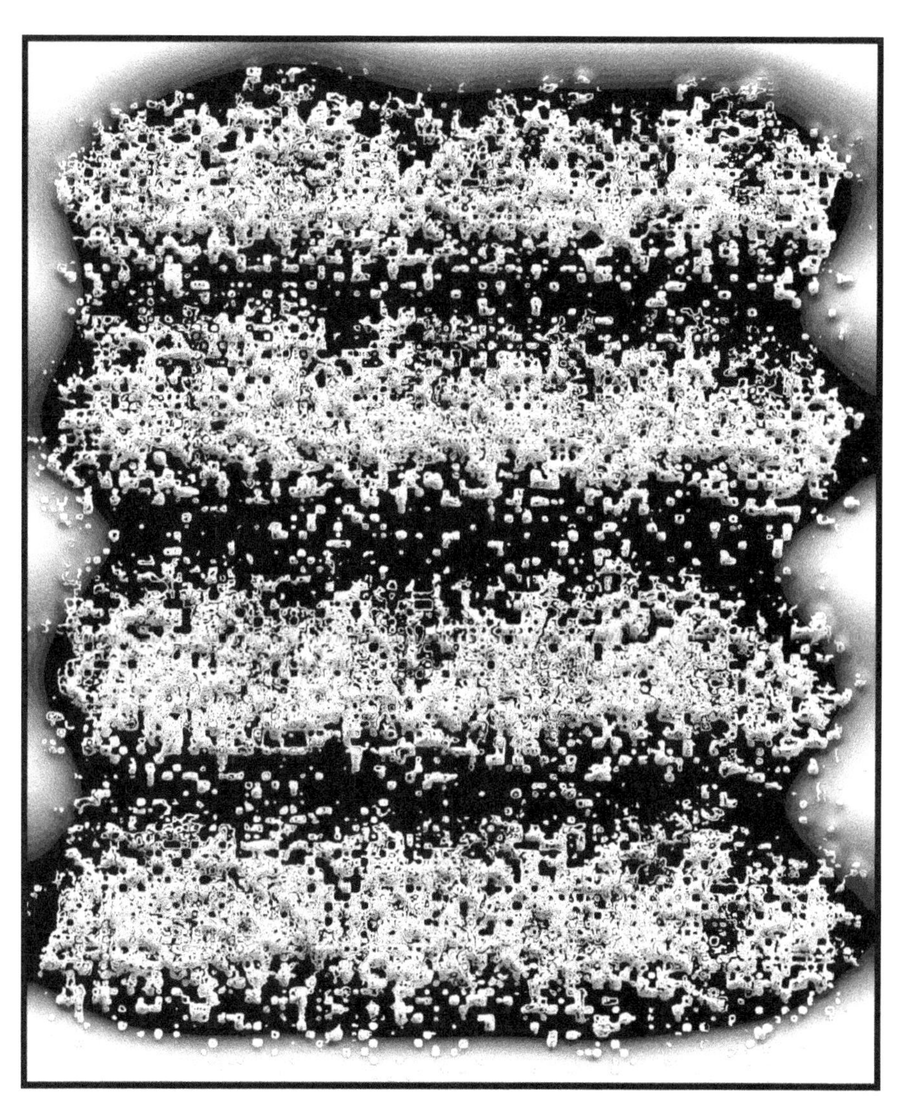

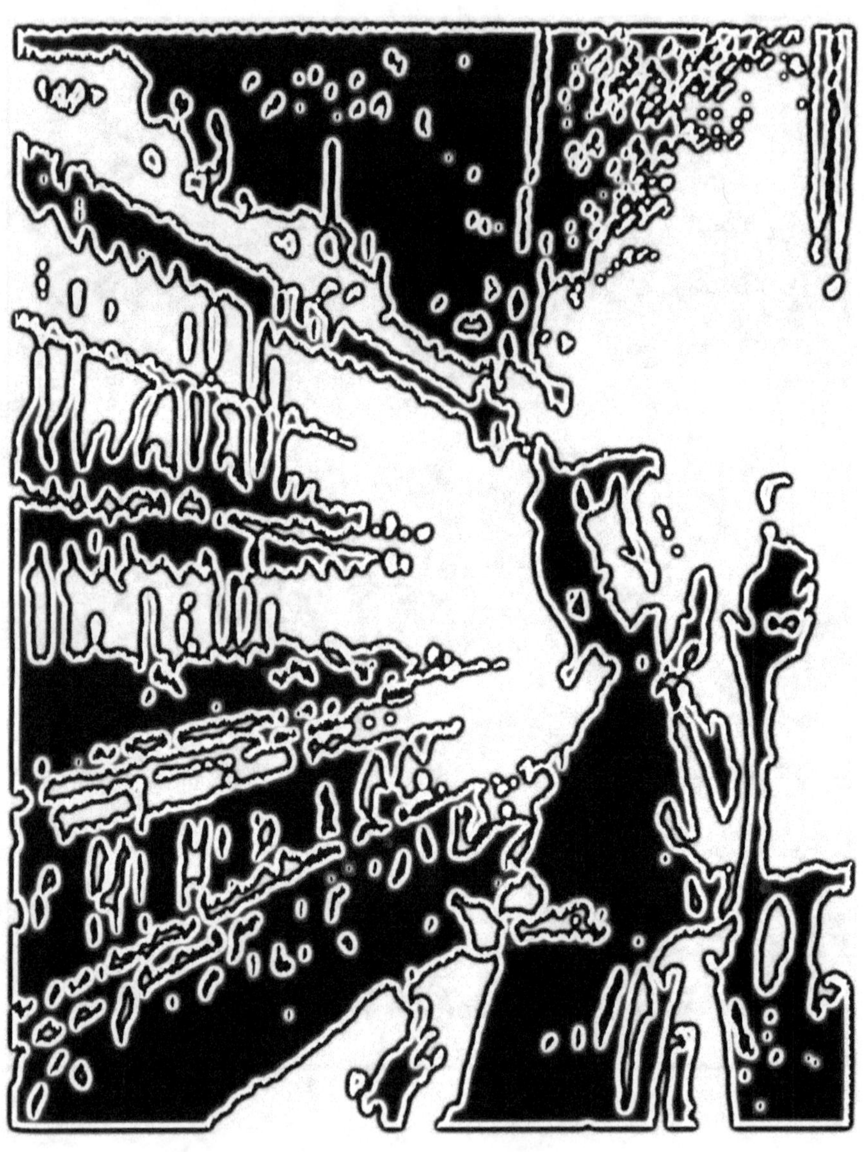

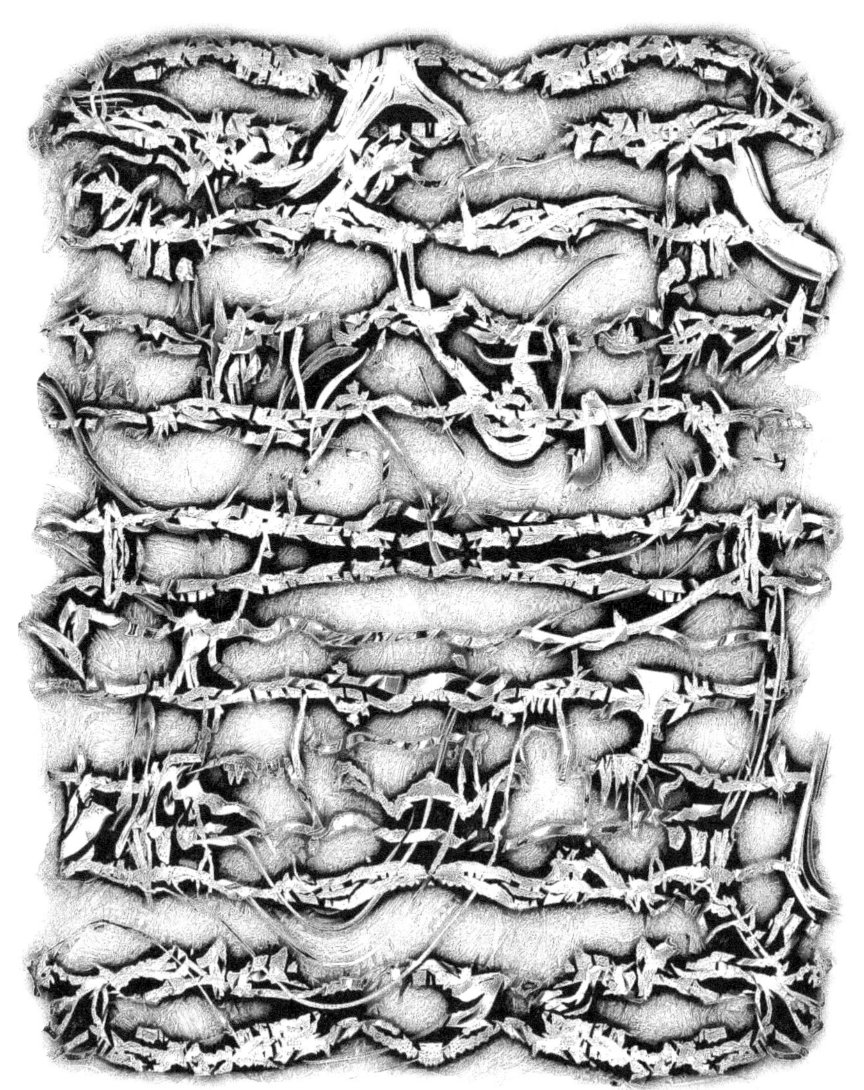

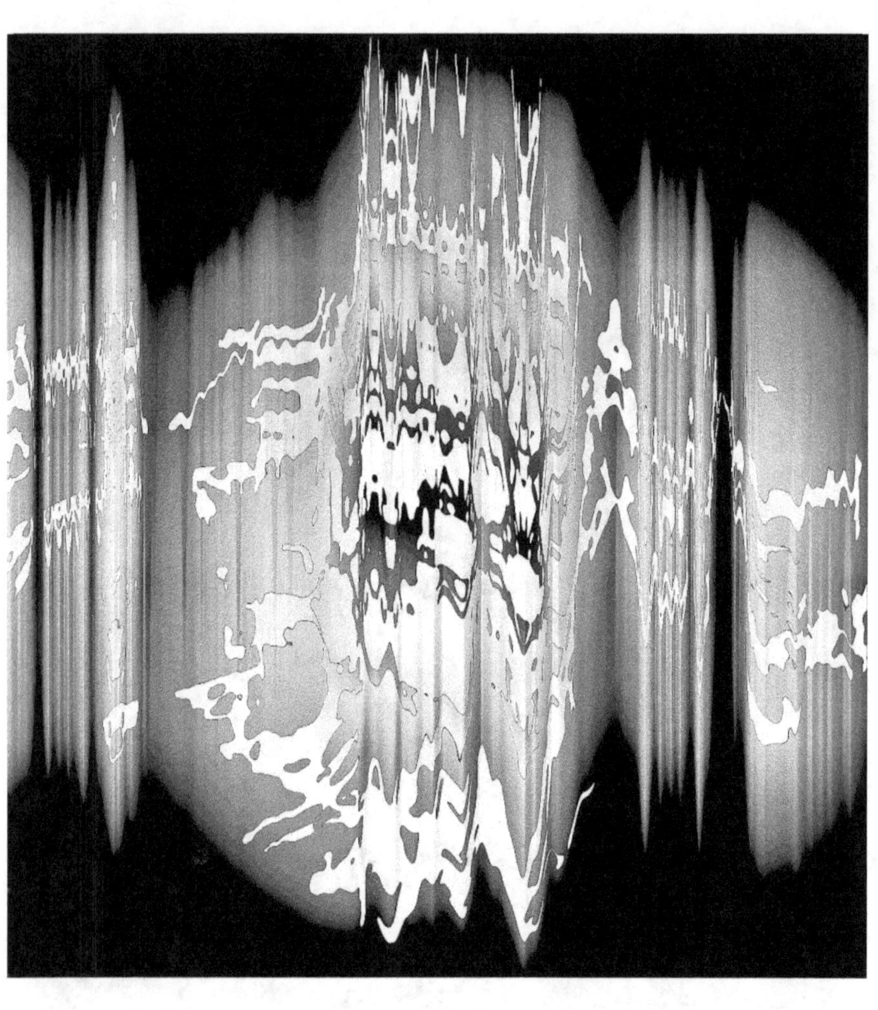

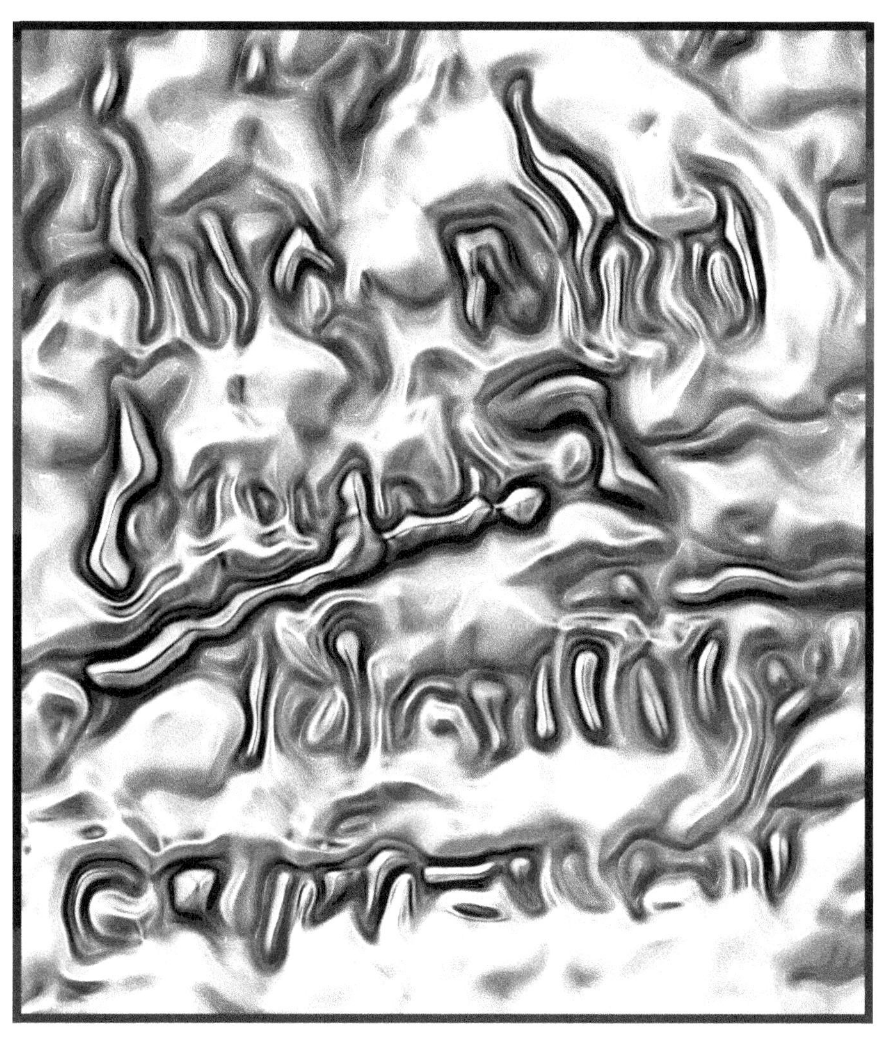

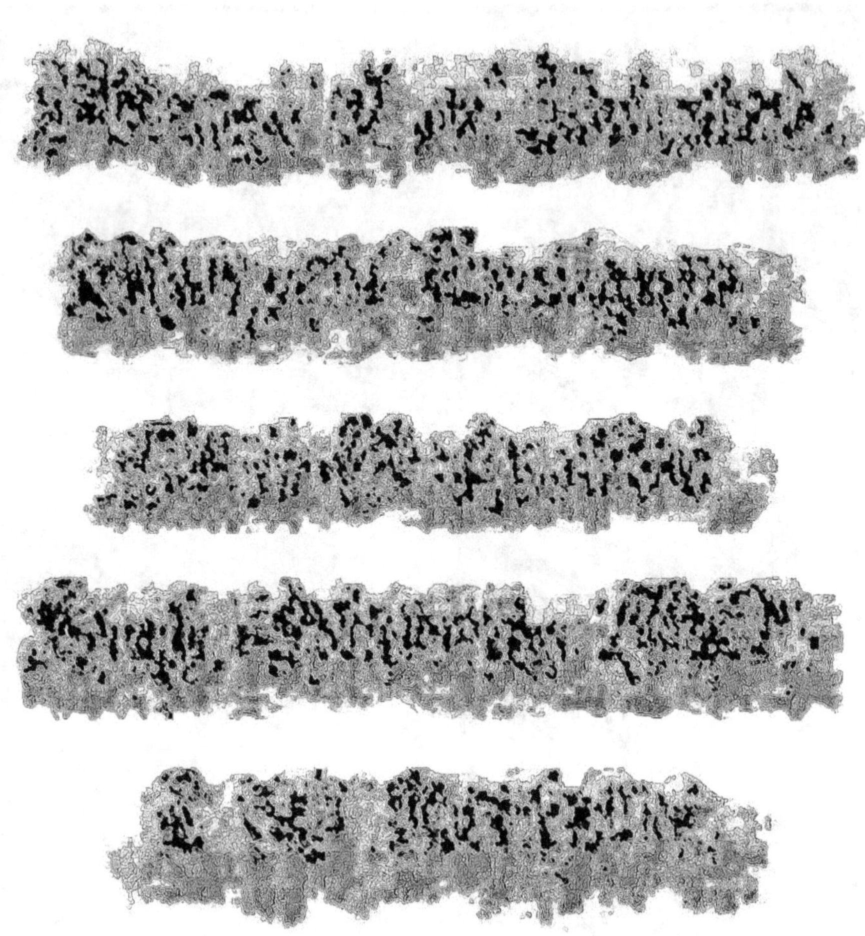

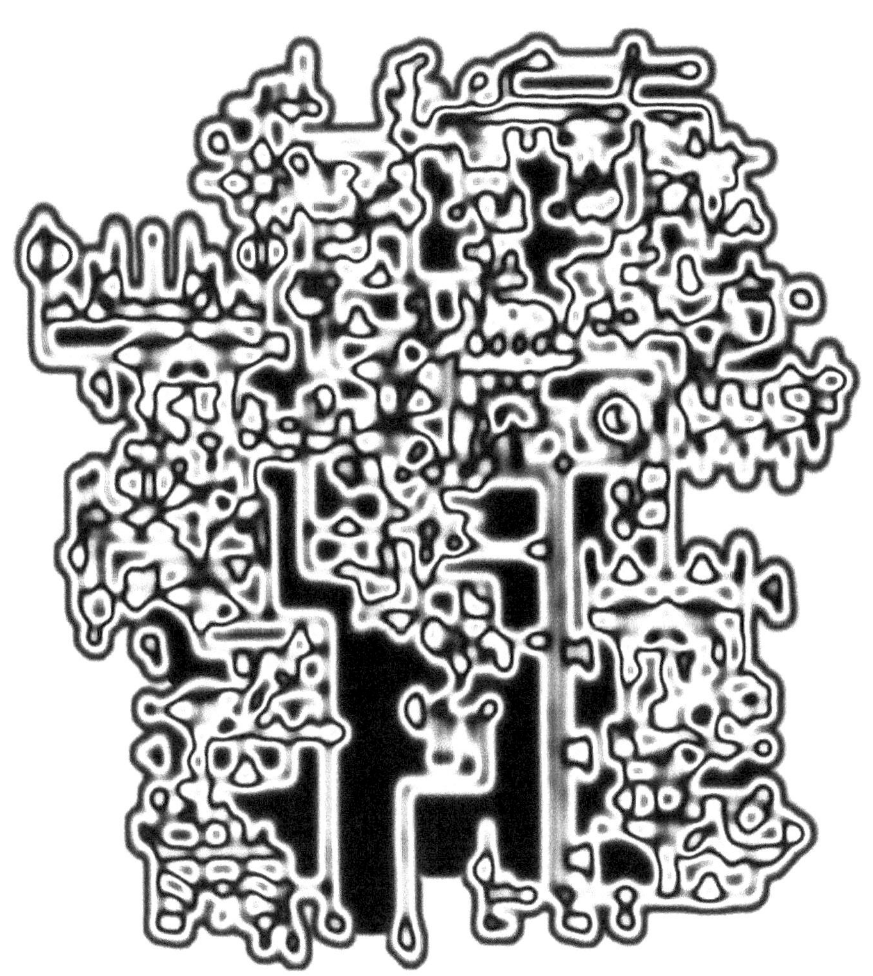

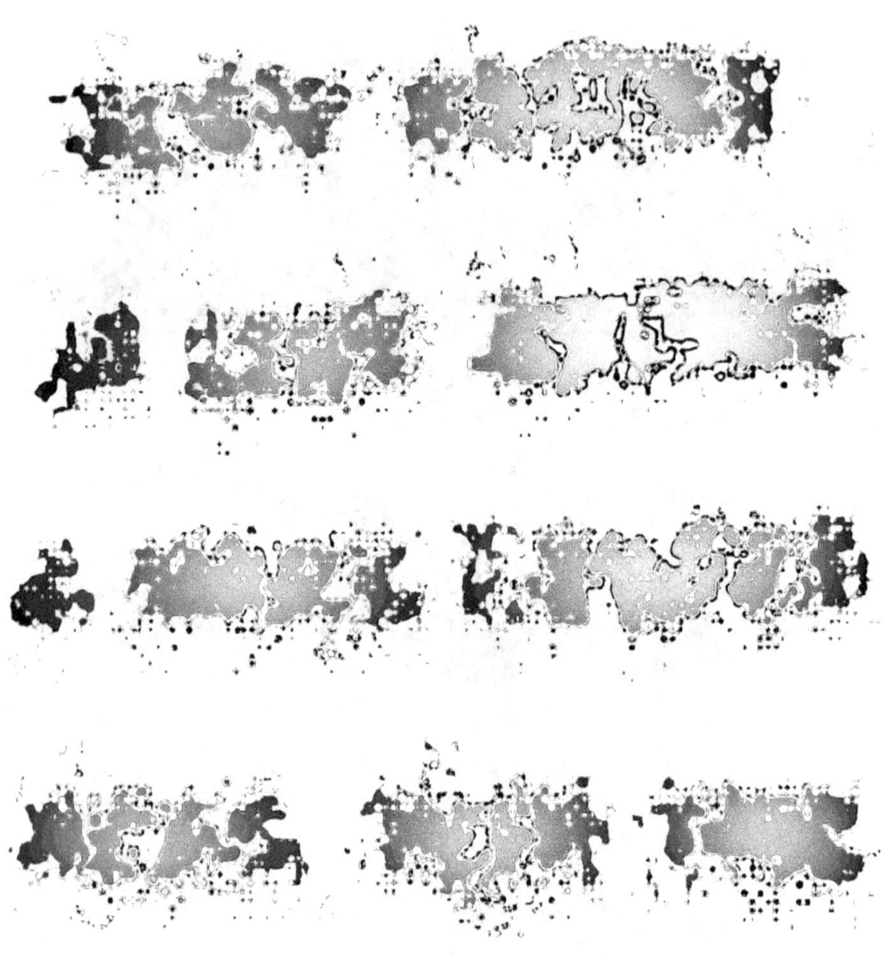

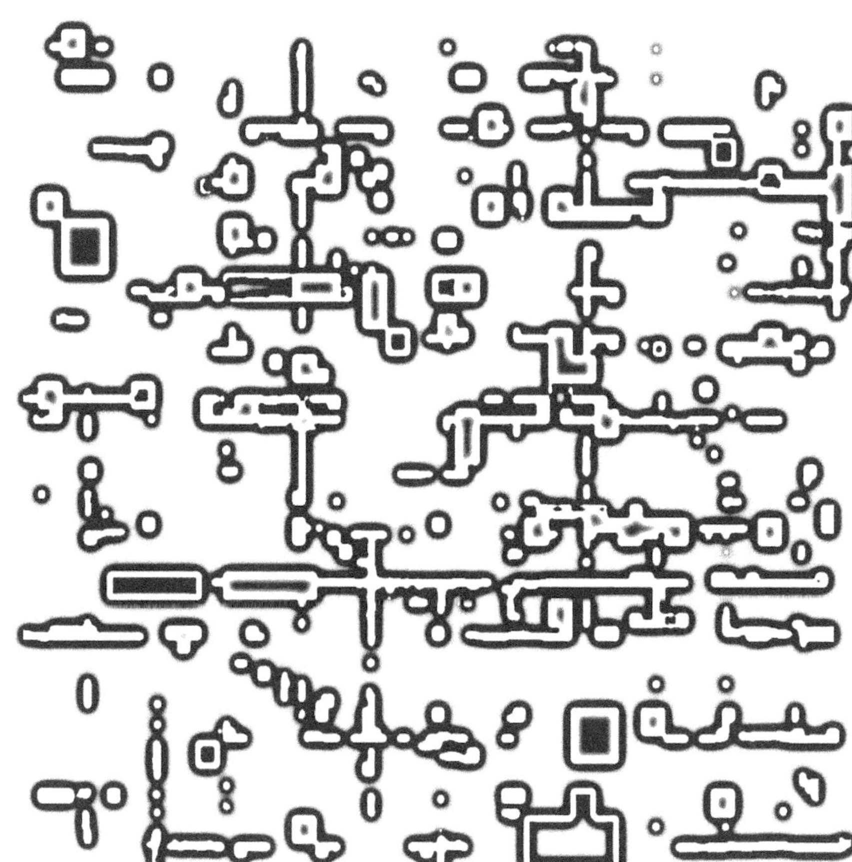

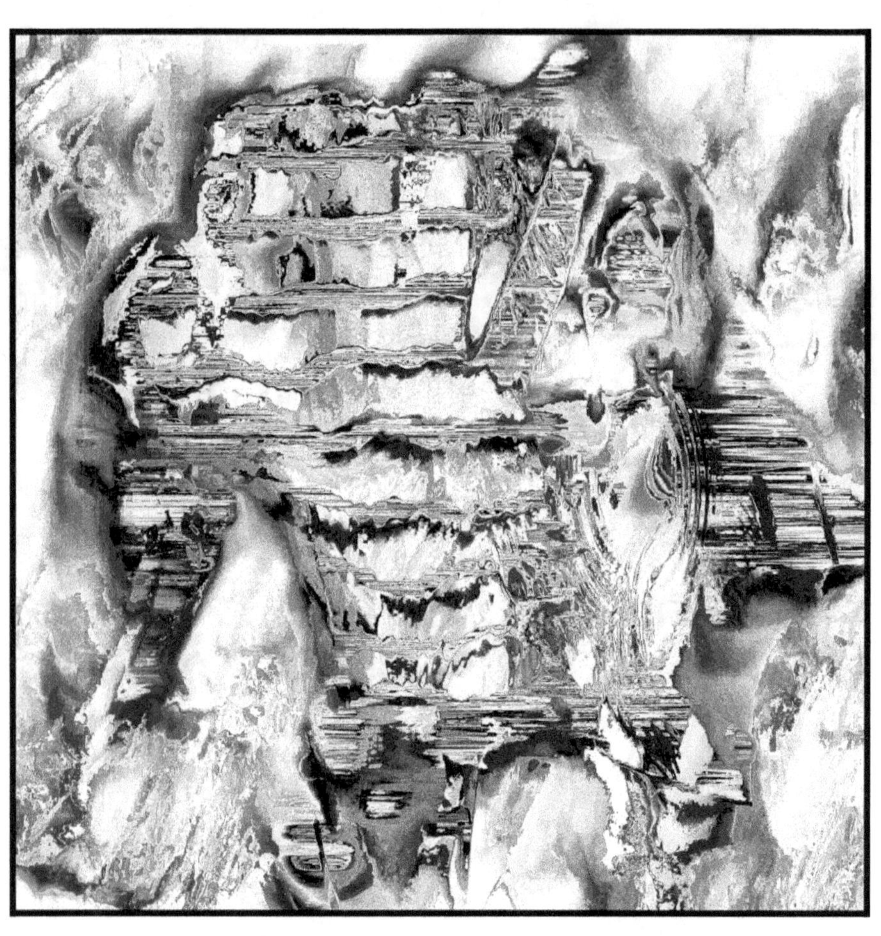

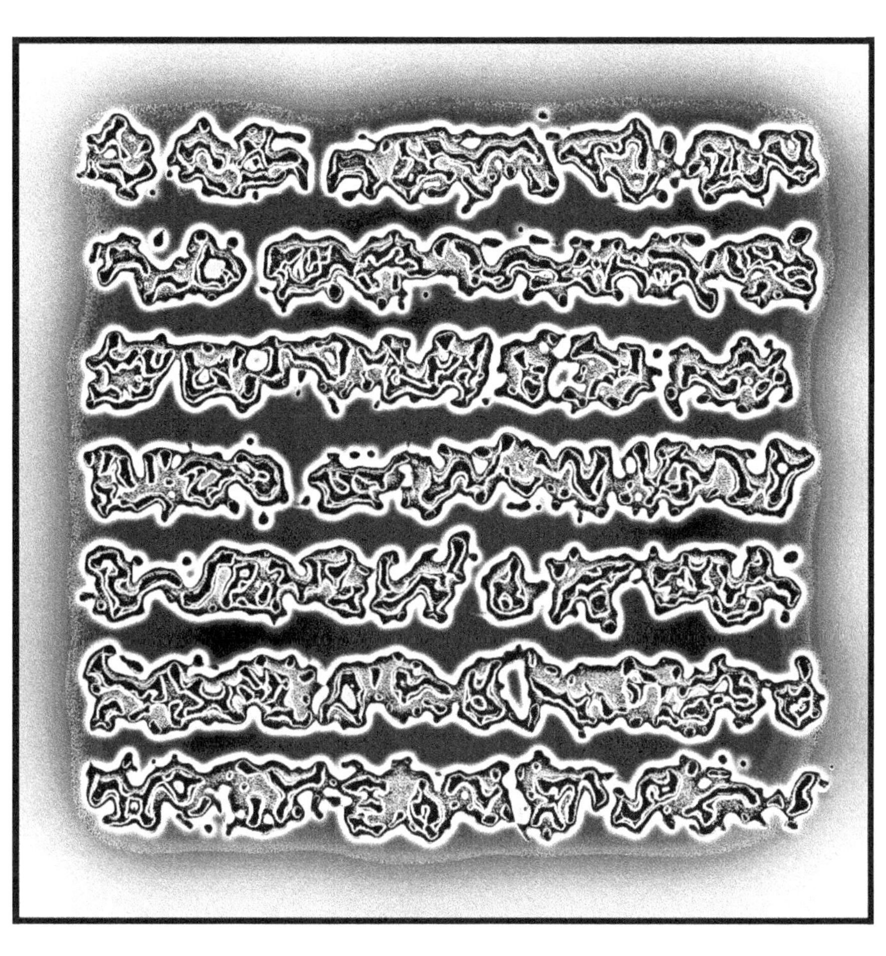

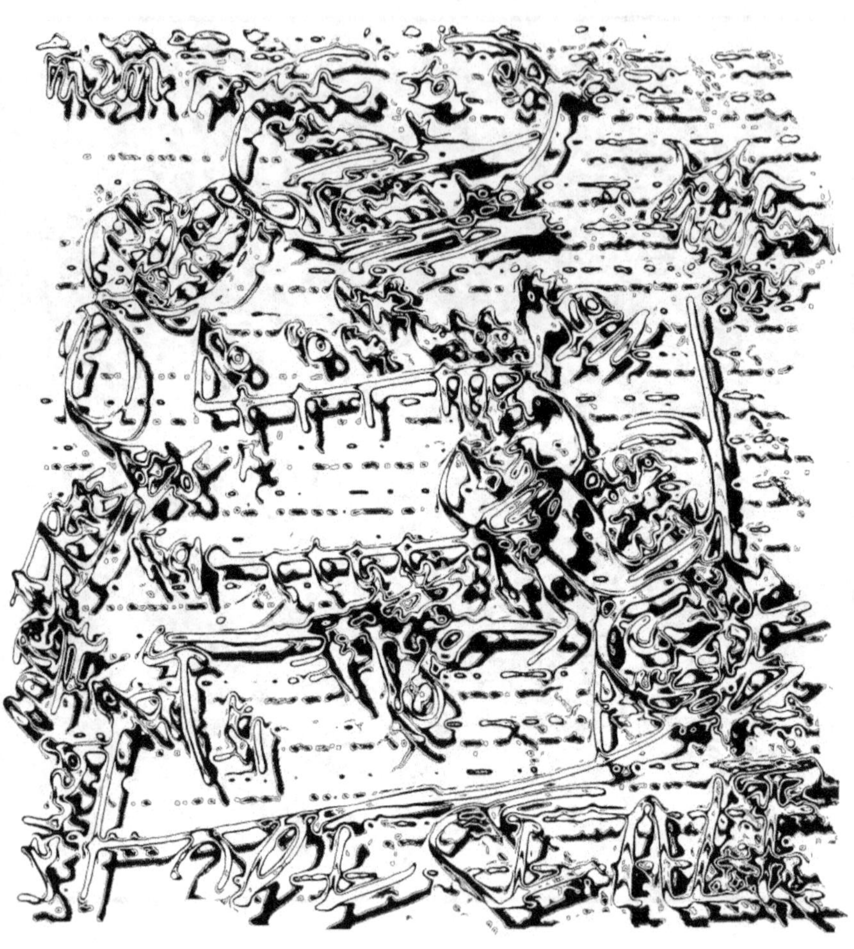

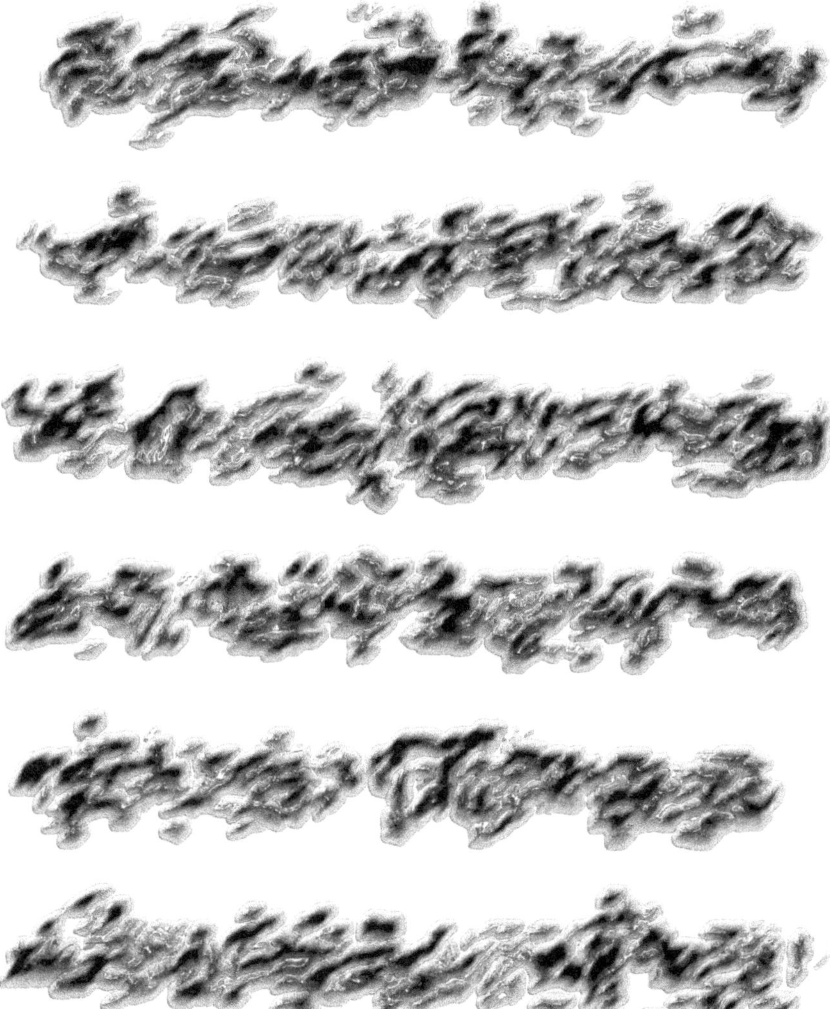

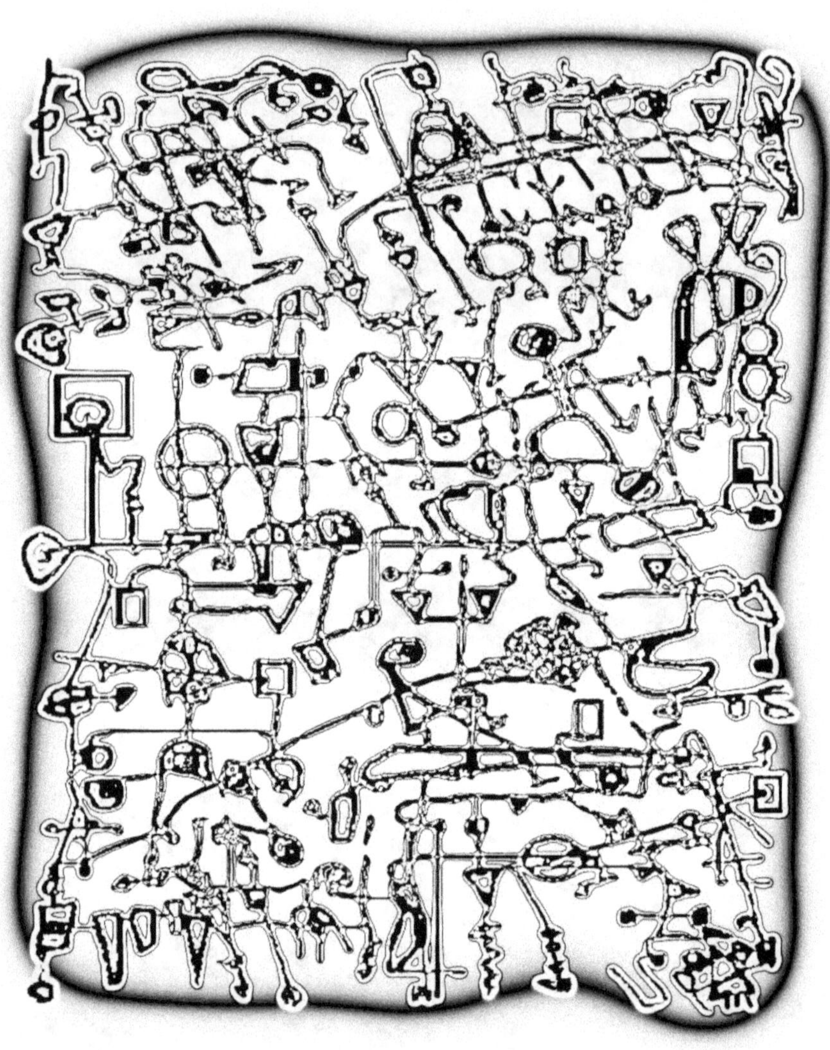

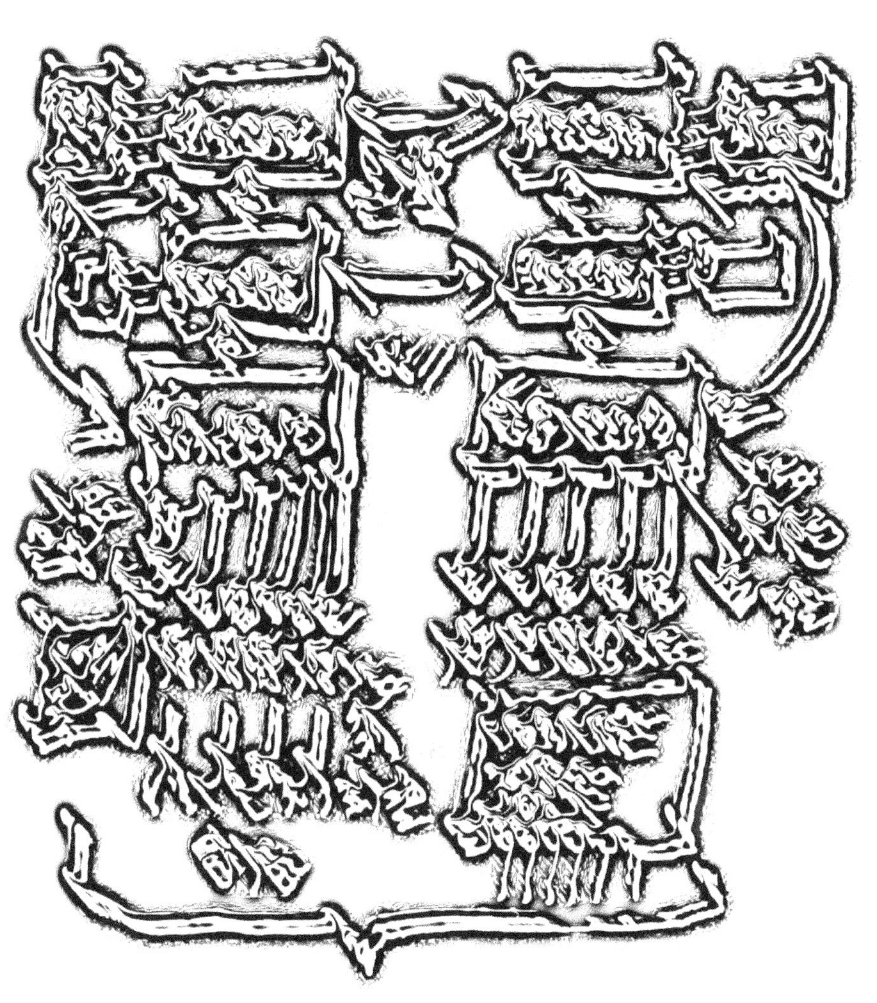

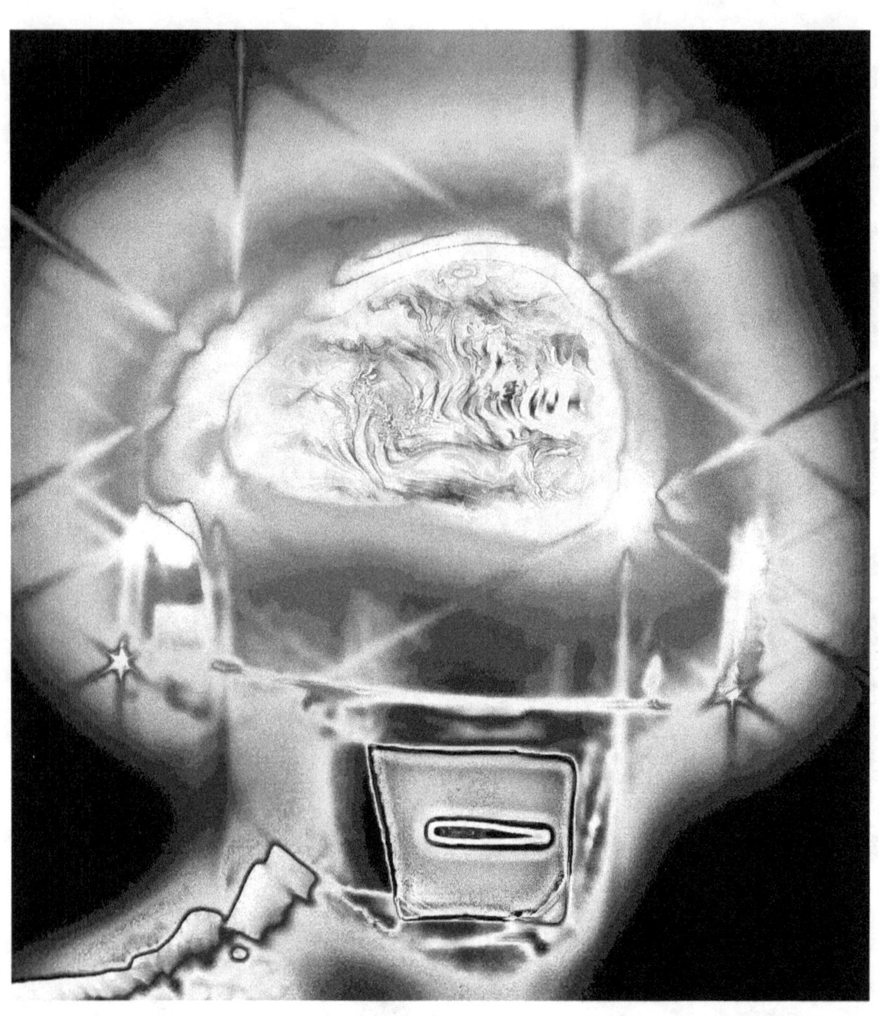

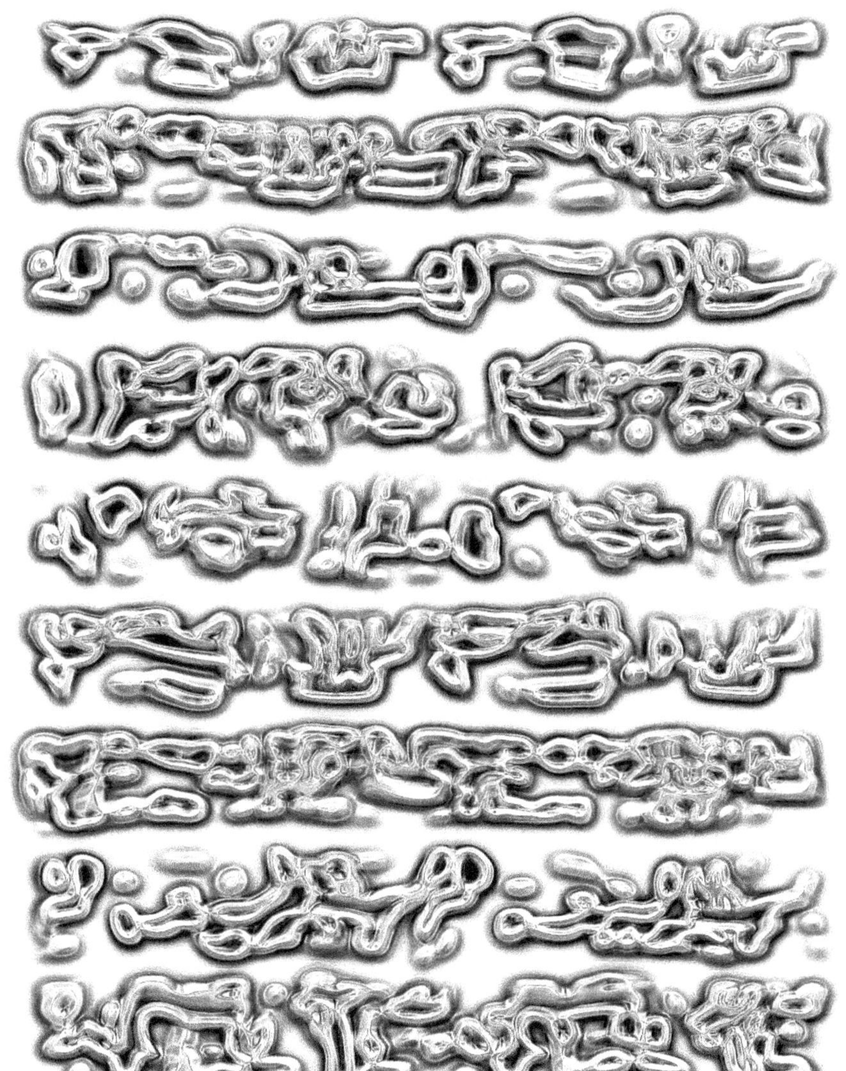

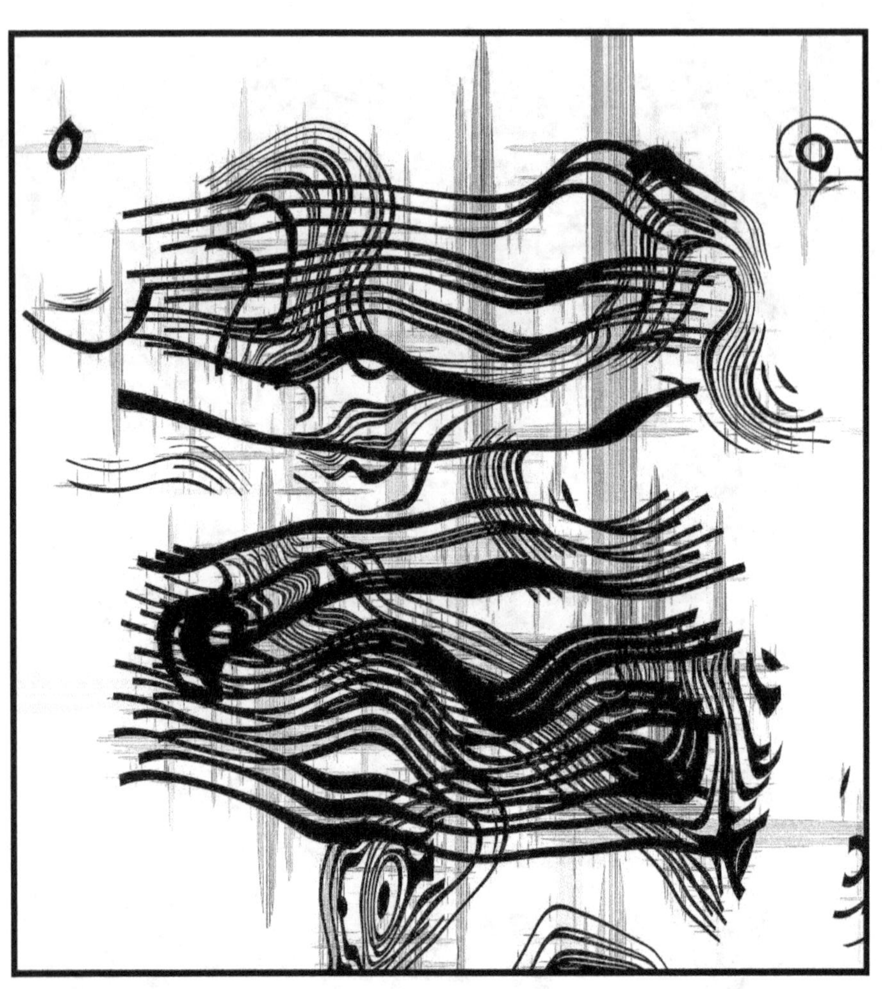

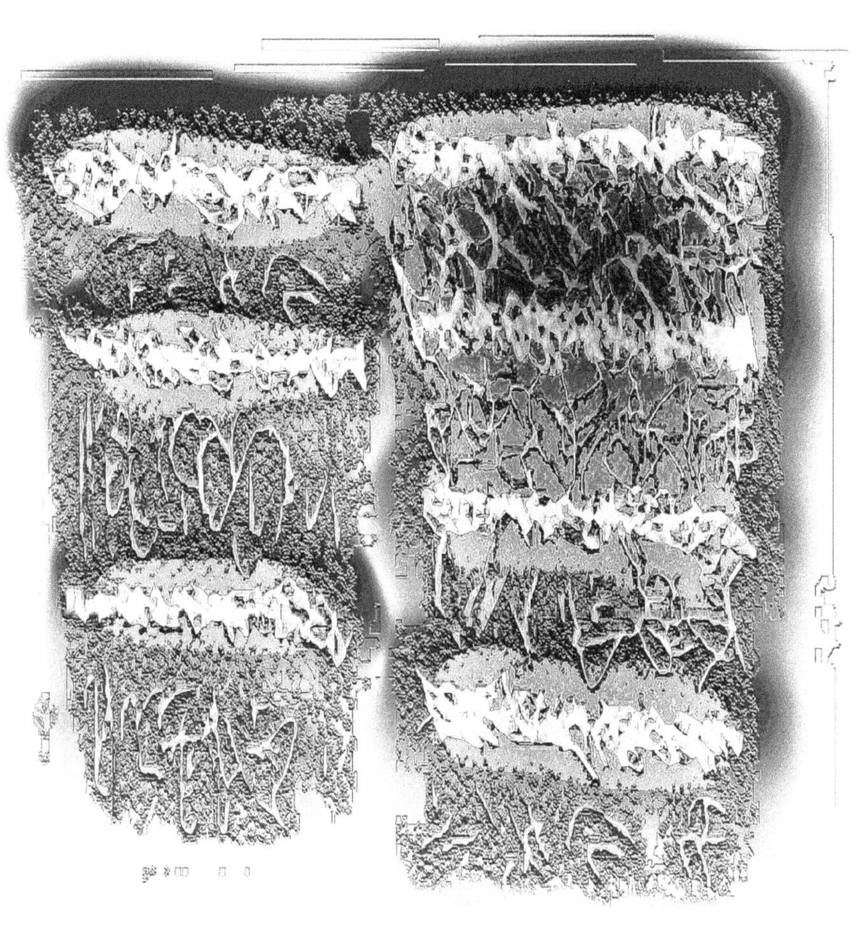

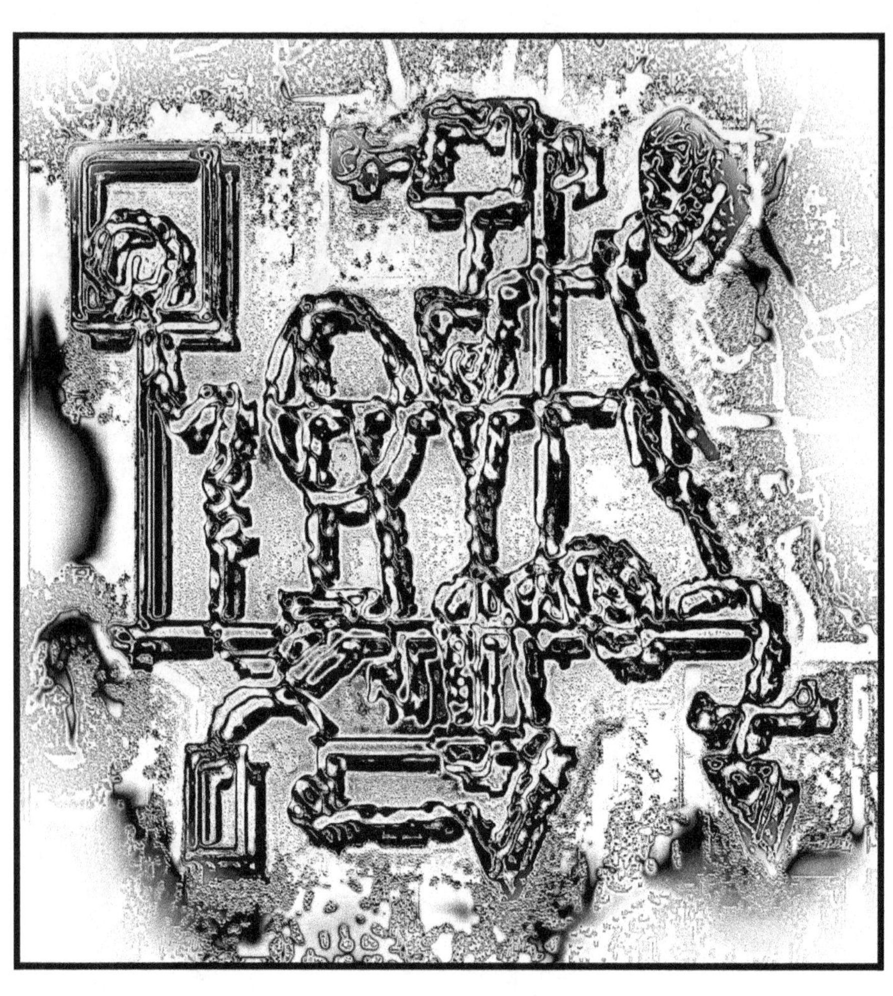

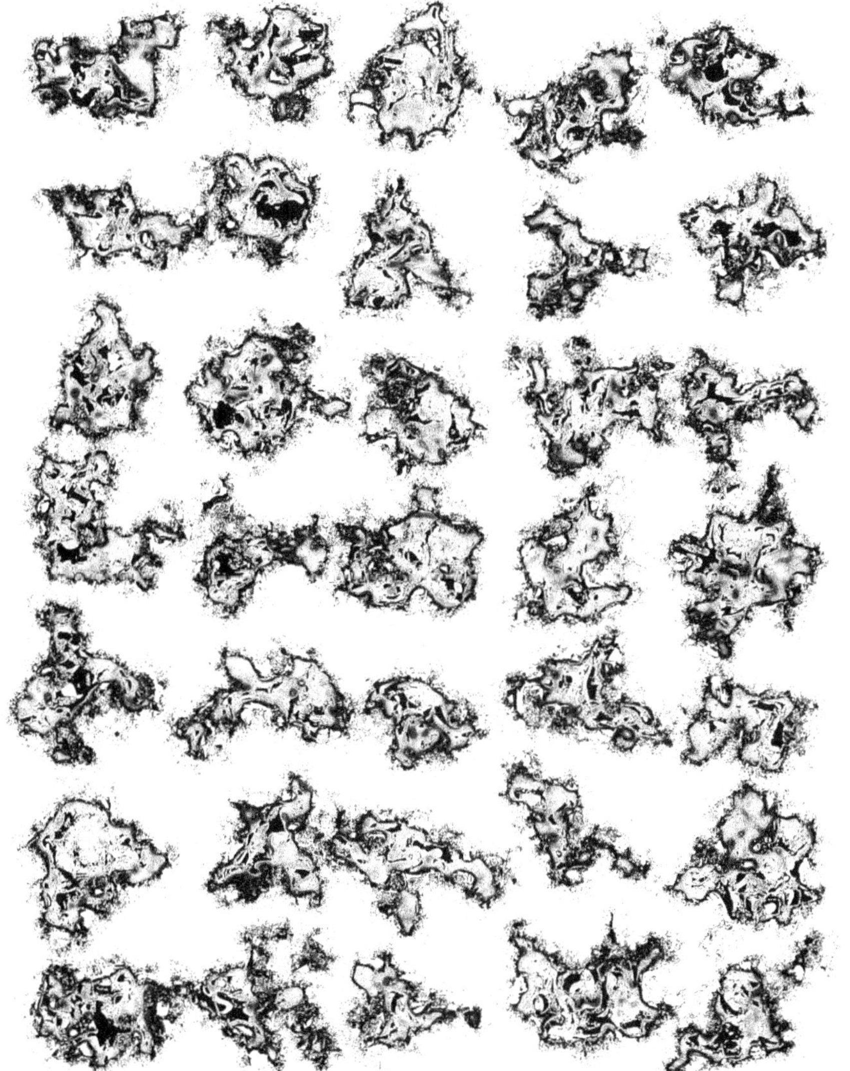

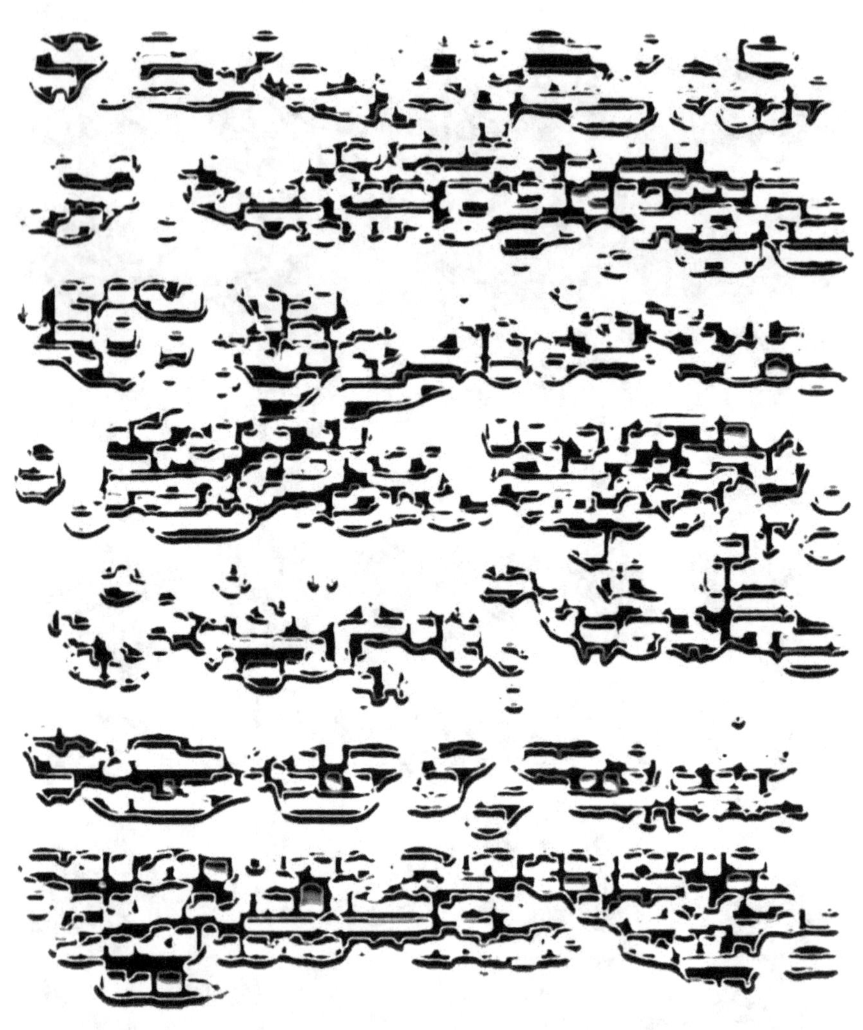

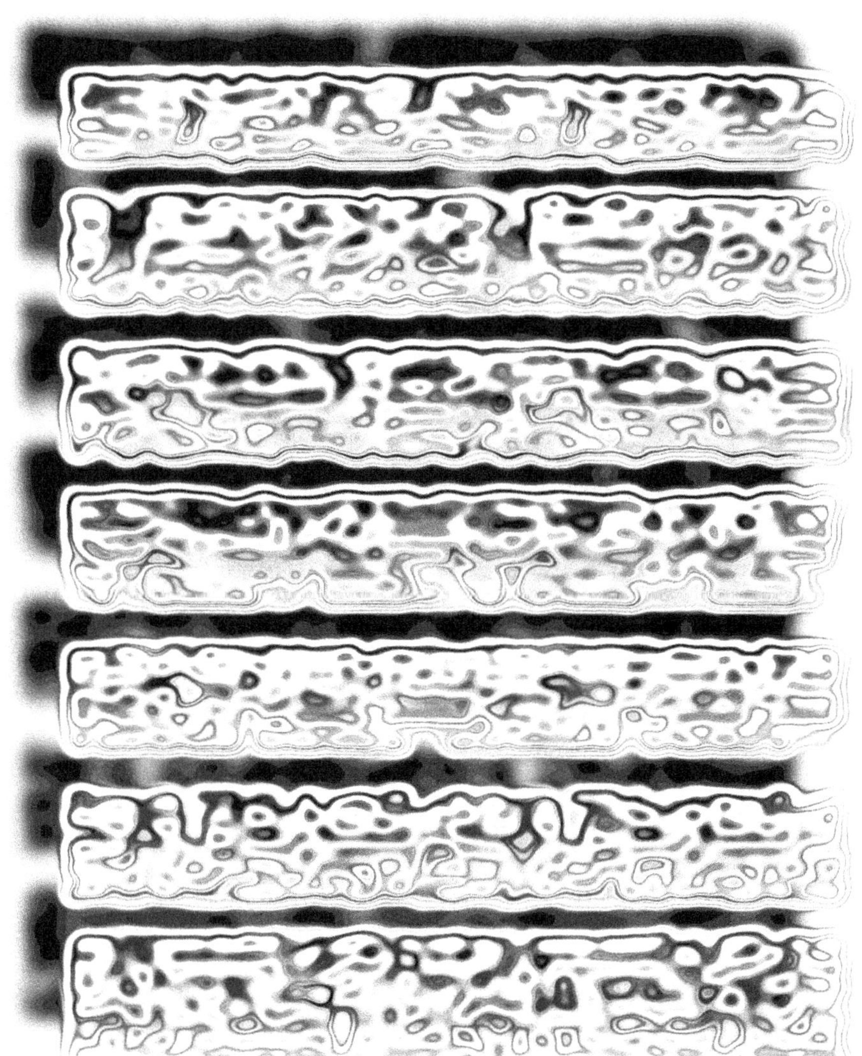

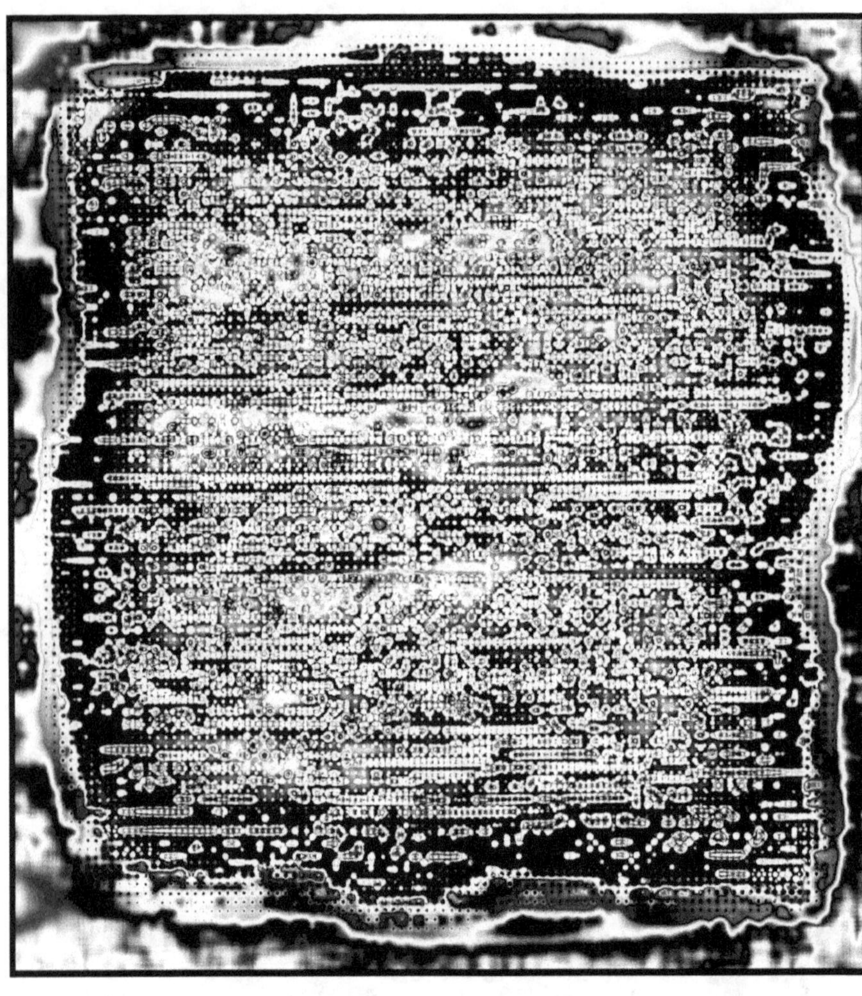

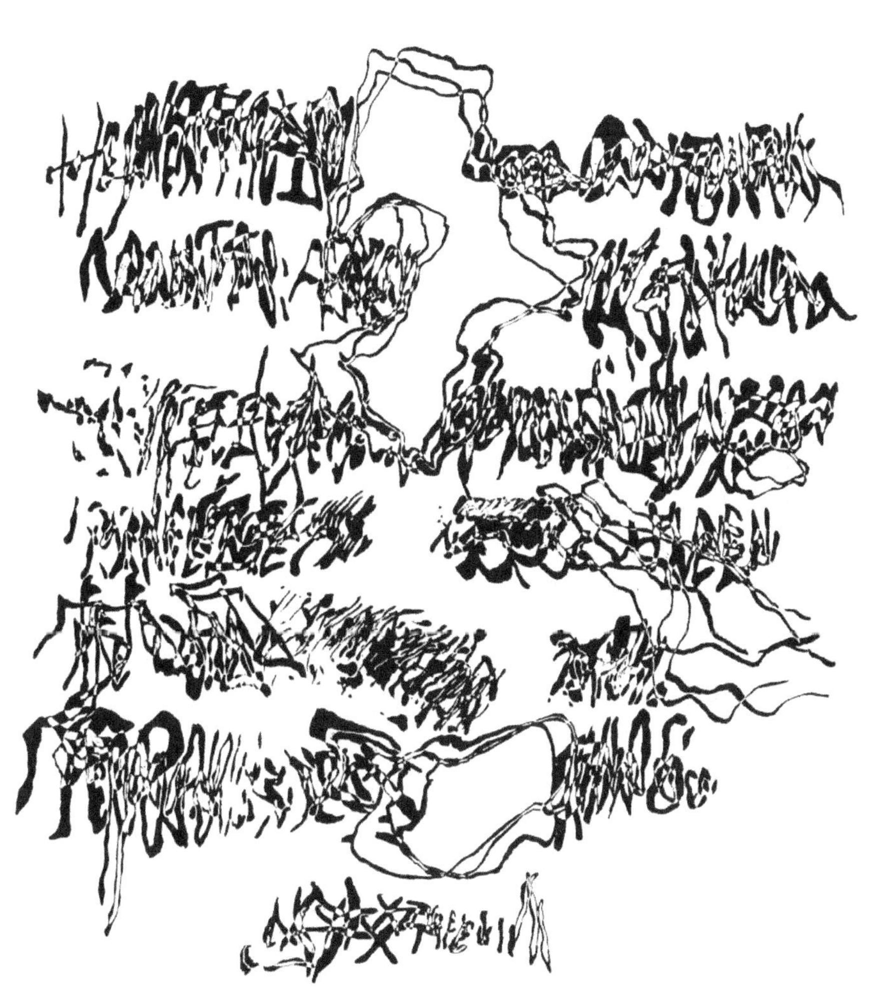

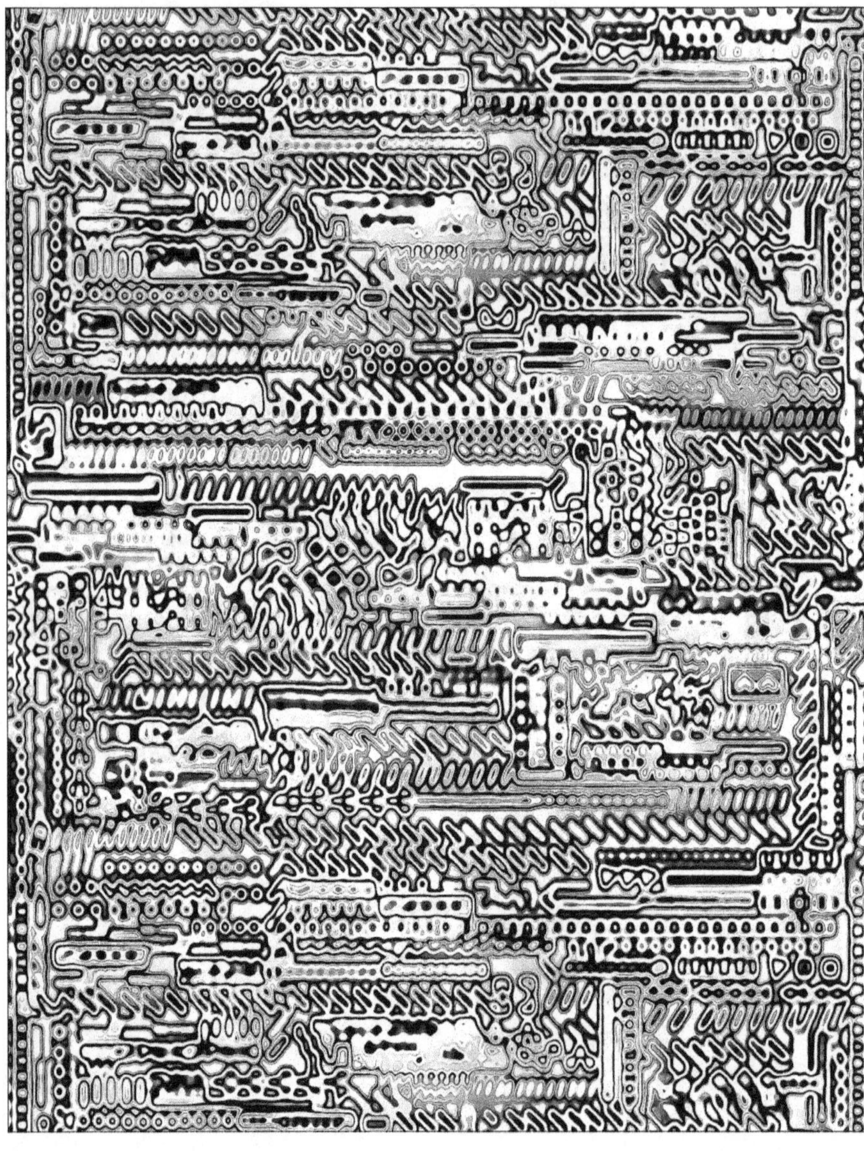

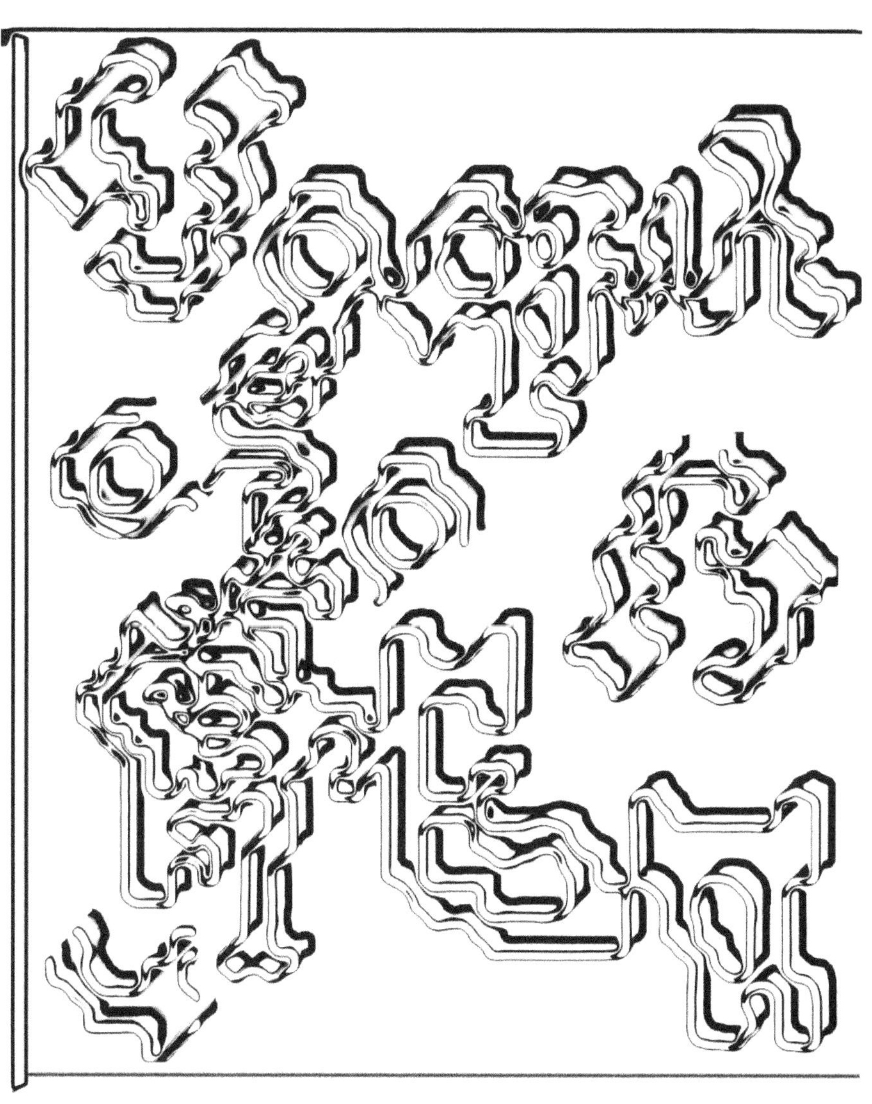

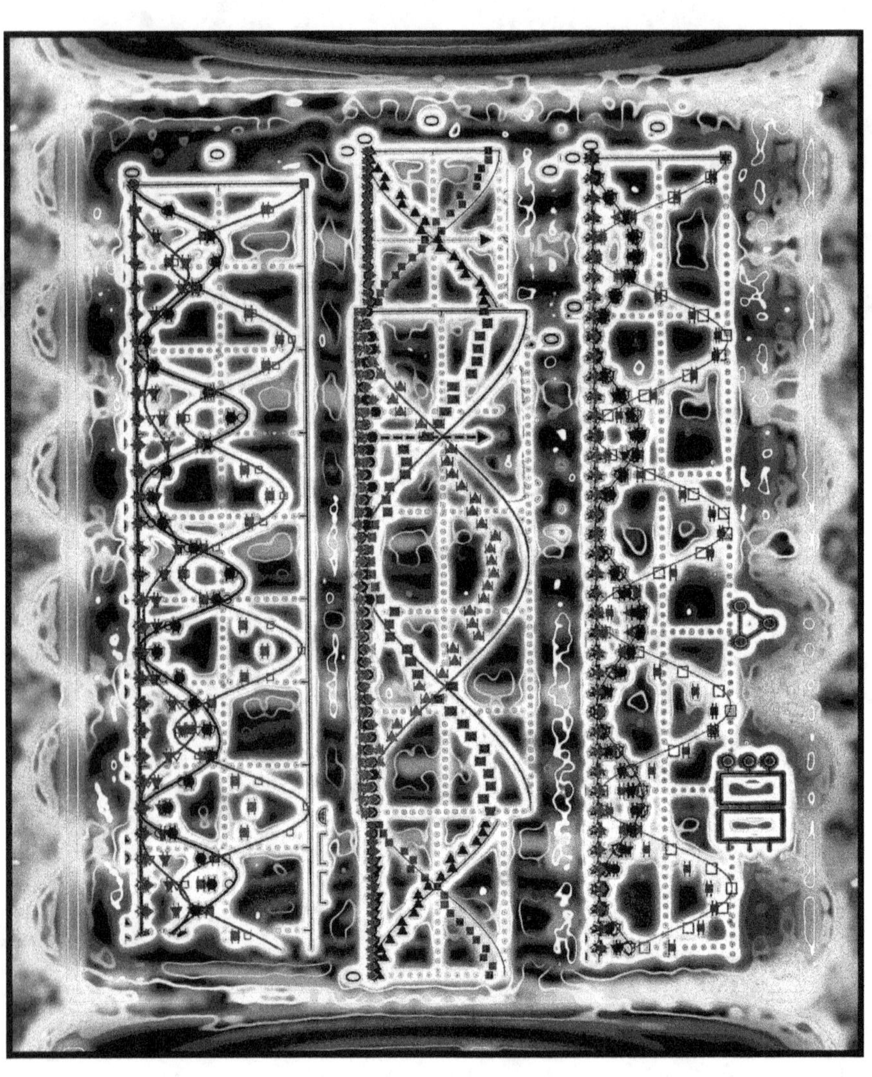

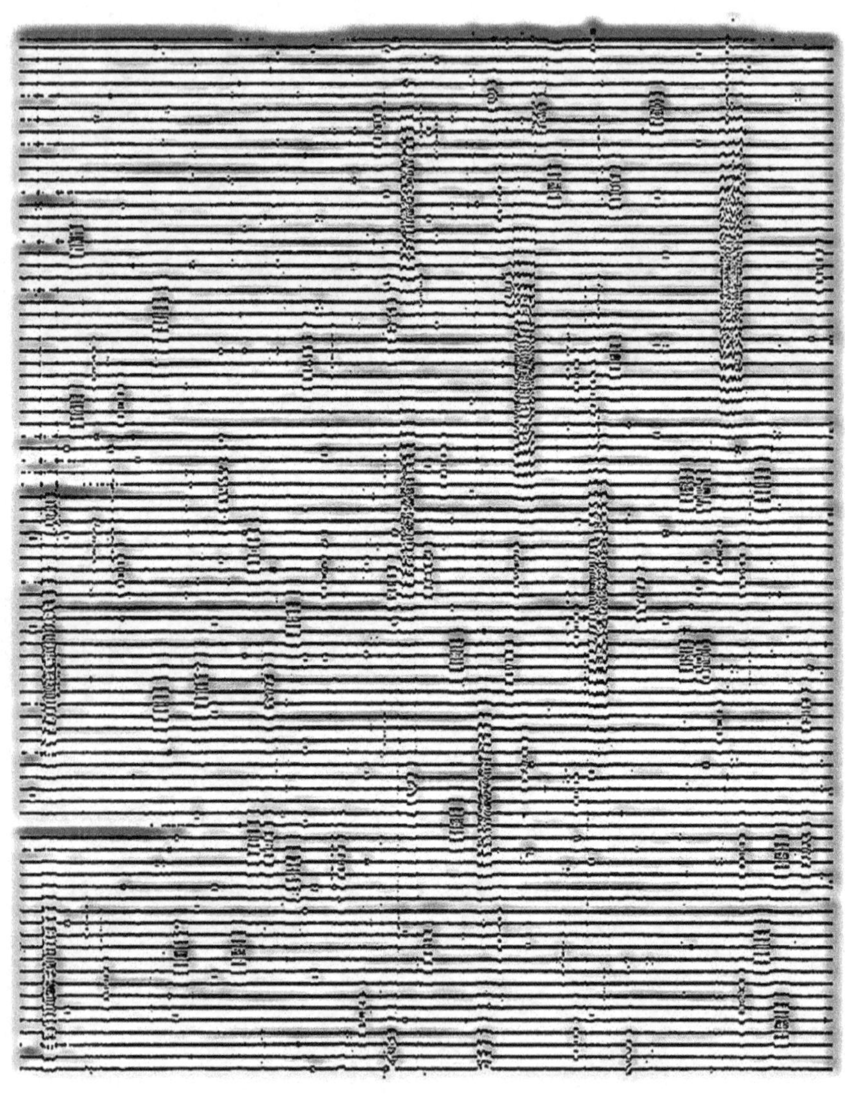

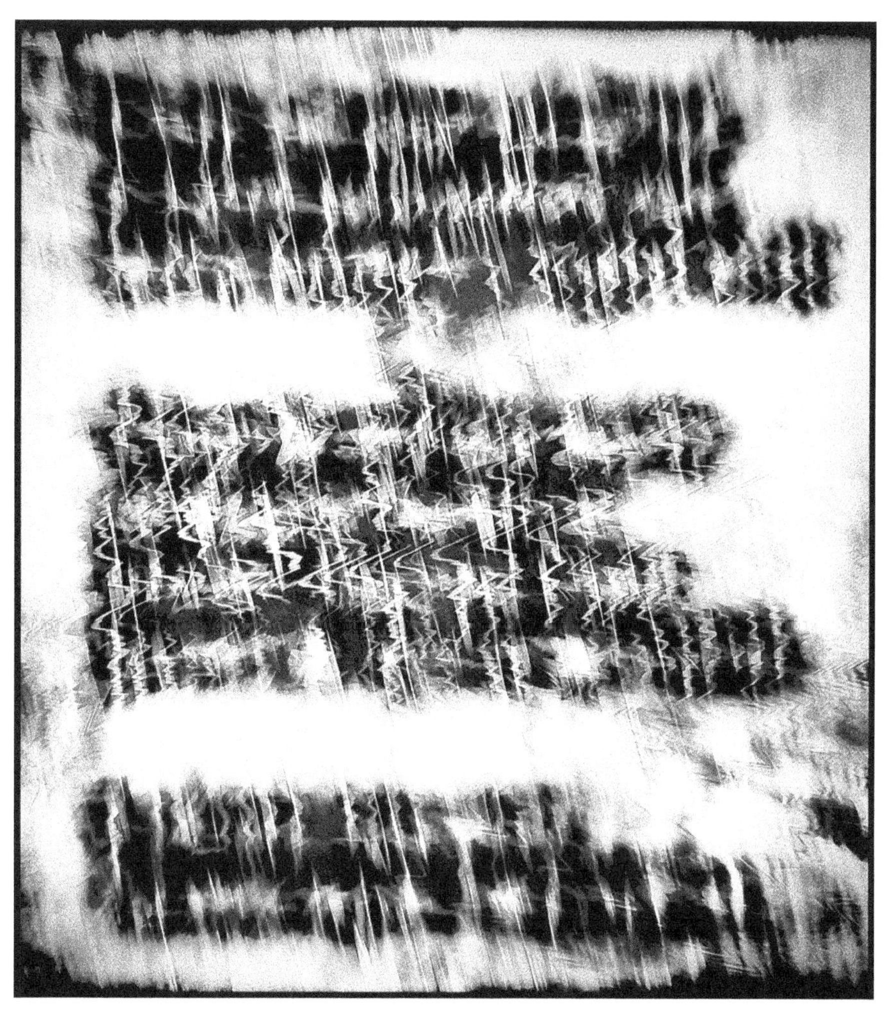

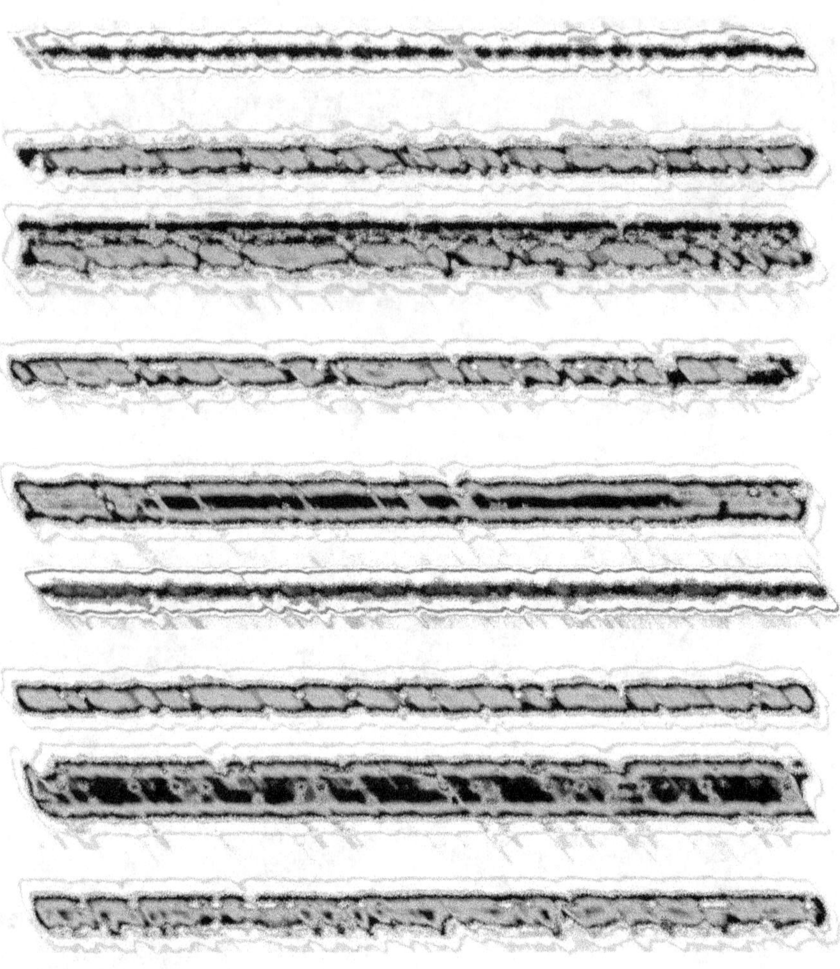

About the Author

Poet, artist and film historian, Spencer Selby (Oct 3rd 1947-April 2nd 2018) has performed work and presented slide shows in many North American cities and in Europe. He is the author of nine poetry books, five collections of visual poetry and two reference works on film noir. Selby ran the Canessa Park Gallery Series in San Francisco, co-edited the visual poetry magazine Score and was a curating member of Glitch Artists Collective.

http://www.selbysart.com/

www.ingramcontent.com/pod-product-compliance
Lightning Source LLC
LaVergne TN
LVHW020640100826
845148LV00012B/2262

* 9 7 8 1 7 3 2 8 7 8 8 2 2 *